The Maine
LOBSTER
Book

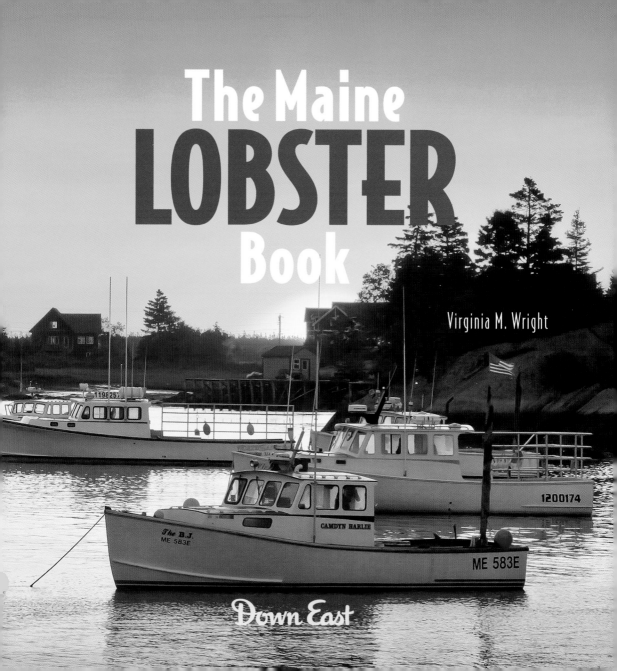

The Maine LOBSTER Book

Virginia M. Wright

Down East

ISBN: 978-1-60893-041-8

Design by Lynda Chilton
Front cover photograph by StockFood America/Thom DeSanto

Library of Congress Cataloging-in-Publication Data

Wright, Virginia (Virginia M.)
  The Maine lobster book / Virginia M. Wright.
      p. cm.
  ISBN 978-1-60893-041-8
1. American lobster. 2. Cooking (Lobsters) I. Title.
  TX754.L63W75 2012
  641.6'95--dc23

                              2012003485

Printed in China
5 4 3 2 1

BOOKS·MAGAZINE·ONLINE
w w w . d o w n e a s t . c o m

Distributed to the trade by National Book Network

"A truly
destitute man
is not one
without riches,
but the poor
wretch who has
never partaken
of lobster."

— Anonymous

Crustacean Contents

Eat 94

Welcome to Lobster Land

**iStock Photo/
Joachim Angeltun**

Homarus americanus — American lobster — is fished from New Jersey to Labrador, but it takes on iconic status in Maine, and for good reason: Lobsters are everywhere.

No, they're not literally skittering over the sidewalks, snapping their great claws at passersby, but they, and all the paraphernalia involved in catching, cooking, and serving them, are so deeply interwoven into the sights and sounds of the Maine coast that it is almost impossible to imagine what would remain if they suddenly disappeared.

Consider: A stroll down Main Street in a coastal village of any consequence from Kittery to Eastport finds restaurants serving lobster steamed, stewed, baked, stuffed into rolls, casseroled, and ladled atop pasta. Lobsters find their way into paintings and posters on art gallery walls, and their claws, rendered in 18-carat gold, clasp diamonds, and pearls, in jewelry store windows. Whimsical lobster sculptures stand like doormen at store entries, and the crustaceans provide endless inspiration for souvenir makers (lobster boxer shorts, anyone?).

And that's just scratching the surface. Amble down any of Maine's peninsulas and you'll encounter lobster traps stacked high in yard after yard. Weathered dealer and bait sheds sit atop piers stretching into harbors dotted with lobsterboats — unless, of course, the lobstermen are out fishing, in which case you see them offshore, moving from buoy to buoy and pulling traps under a cloud of darting seagulls. The ever-present rumble of their engines cuts through the ocean's din.

What follows is an informative, fun, and useful guide for the lobster lover — to learn, live, and eat everything Maine lobster. Don't forget your bib!

Ginny

If all you know about lobster is your unwavering claim that the tail tastes best, be prepared to be amazed by these peculiar creatures. The science behind these "bugs" of the ocean, from their steamy sex lives to the surprising products made from their discarded shells, is almost as tasty as their meat.

{ LEARN }

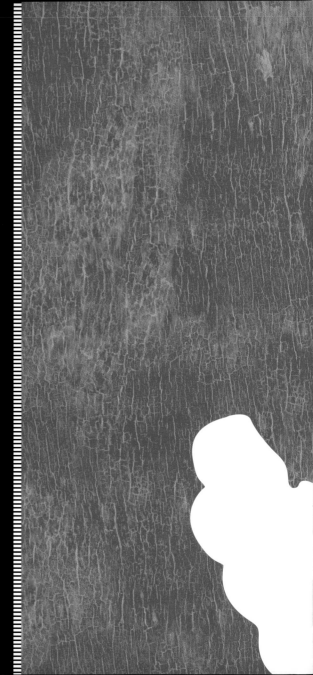

Shutterstock/Mark Skainy

Sure, lobstering takes place elsewhere, but the fishery is at its richest and densest in Maine. And with record catches year after year for the past twenty years,

Lobster Landings

the lobster's importance to Maine's economy and culture is growing. In 2011, Maine lobster landings topped 100 million pounds, valued at more than $300 million — that's nearly 90 percent of the lobster landings in the Northeast, where it is the most valuable fishery, and slightly less than half of all North American landings (Canadian lobster landings average between 110 and 120 million pounds).

Maine lobster landings are at an all-time high — in 2011, the catch exceeded 100 million pounds, which is five times the historical average.

The total economic impact of the fishery — that includes boat builders, marine suppliers, fuel and bait dealers, and tourism — exceeds $500 million in Maine.

"In many ways, now is the best of times for lobstering," says Carl Wilson, the state of Maine's chief lobster biologist, who monitors lobster populations and provides guidance for managing the fishery. "It's never been so good, and there's never been so much money coming in. We have a good conservation ethic within the fishery, and we have all this science that says the lobster population appears to be in great shape. But it's also never been more precarious because the failure of other fisheries,

A shortage of herring, the traditional lobster bait, has intensified the search for alternatives.

Lynda Chilton

iStock Photo/Jan Tyler

whether due to mismanagement or environmental changes, has left us with just this one horse. Many of these coastal communities would be at extreme risk if lobstering were to hiccup."

Several theories have been advanced to explain why Maine lobster landings quadrupled over the past twenty years while other fisheries were collapsing. Indeed, some scientists believe the very decline of those fisheries may have benefited lobster by reducing predators like cod and haddock.

Climate change has been implicated as well. While warmer water temperatures are blamed for plummeting lobster populations in waters south of Cape Cod, the water has warmed just enough in the Gulf of Maine to actually benefit lobsters, Wilson says.

Maine's conservation efforts — the strictest of any lobster fishery — also may be playing a role in creating healthy lobster stocks. Key among these are size limits and V-notching. Lobstermen cannot keep lobsters whose carapace is less than 3 ¼ inches long or more than 5 inches long, a practice that ensures each animal reaches an age where it is capable of at least one reproduction cycle and protects

Maine's strict conservation efforts get some of the credit for the gargantuan lobster catches of recent years.

iStock Photo/Natalia Bratslavsky

mature lobsters that have a greater capacity for breeding and reproduction. V-notching, meanwhile, is aimed at protecting the brood stock. Lobstermen notch a "V" into the tail fin of any egg-bearing lobster found in a trap and toss her back into the sea. That notch protects her as long as she has it, whether she is carrying eggs or not.

This animal-by-animal assessment by fishermen distinguishes lobstering from other fisheries, Wilson points out. "There's both a biological component and a social component in that the assumption is you're going to get something back from that action in the future," he says. "The lobster goes back into the ocean alive and it can be caught again. That's a unique luxury."

Other conservation measures include license limits (Maine issues 6,000 commercial lobstering licenses annually; about 4,500 harvesters are fishing full time), trap limits (800 traps per license holder), and traps with biodegradable panels that dissolve over time, allowing lobsters to escape from a derelict trap. ❖

Lobstermen measure every lobster they catch — and toss back any animals that are too big or too small.

Lobster Lovemaking

A lady lobster knows what she wants, and what she wants is the guy with a reputation for toughness and strength, the guy all the other lobsters in the neighborhood fear and respect. So she woos him. She leaves gifts — urchins, mussels, sea stars — at his front door. When she has his attention, she boldly moves in. And once they are better acquainted

— a few days perhaps — she shimmies out of her tight suit of armor, exposing herself in all her soft, naked vulnerability. Summoning her strength (molting is an exhausting affair that leaves her limp as a strand of seaweed for nearly an hour), she raises her antennae to fondle her mate's rostrum, the hornlike projection between his eyes. He reciprocates, his own antennae roaming eagerly over her body. Using his legs, he gently rolls her onto her back and deposits capsules of his sperm into a pocket on her abdomen.

"She's just using him in a way," Diane Cowan, a lobster biologist and founder of the Lobster Conservancy, says wryly of this crustacean courtship. "What she really needs

"She's just using him in a way..."

Lobster biologist Diane Cowan and one of the babies she monitors year after year.

The Lobster Conservancy Photo by Sara L. Ellis

Stud muffin that he is...

is a safe place to molt. In science talk, they call it resource defense polygyny, where a male is defending a resource that the female needs."

Indeed, once the female's new shell is sufficiently hardened, she moves out, having no further use for her mate. Chances are good his sperm will go to waste because, if she is young, the female could well molt again before she releases her eggs, shedding the sperm in the process. Or, she may inflict the ultimate snub, jettisoning her ex's sperm packet into the briny blue should she meet a suitor she fancies more. (Pity not the male lobster. Stud muffin that he is, he likely took on a new housemate soon after his erstwhile partner's departure.)

All of which is surprisingly complicated behavior for the creatures we in Maine have nicknamed "bugs,"

iStock Photo/Yory Frenklakh

not only for their creepy-crawly appearance, but also for their brains — or rather, their lack thereof. Lobsters have primitive nervous systems similar to those of insects, which suggests they are no smarter than a grasshopper. Yet these ancient members of the arthropod class of animals (invertebrates with segmented bodies and exoskeletons of chitin) continue to reveal previously unknown facets of their lives to scientists like Cowan, who has devoted all of her adult life to studying lobsters. They also are capable of acts of cunning.

iStock Photo/Joan Vicent Cantó Roig

Consider, for example, University of New Hampshire zoologist Win Watson's stunning 2003 underwater video that shows lobsters of all shapes and sizes treating a baited trap like a drive-through restaurant. Ninety-three percent of the lobsters that enter the trap gorge themselves on the salted herring, then find their way out, prompting Pat White of the Maine Lobstermen's Association to tell the *Christian Science Monitor,* "It's pretty discouraging to think that here we, as intelligent human beings, have been trying our best to harvest this thing that has no brain to speak of

and they're outsmarting us. But it may be that part of the success of our fishery is due to the fact that our traps are as inefficient as they are." (Watch Professor Watson's videos at the UNH Web site: win.unh.edu/media/movies.html)

Commercially fished for 150 years, the American lobster, or *Homarus americanus,* dwells in the North Atlantic from North Carolina to Labrador and is most plentiful in the Gulf of Maine. Lobsters lead an itinerant lifestyle, determined by the seasons. Late spring and summer finds them dwelling in warmer waters inshore ("warm water" in Maine is fifty-two to sixty-two degrees). Come fall, they migrate to the deeper waters fifteen to forty miles offshore, which is why most Maine lobstermen don't fish in winter — getting to where the lobsters are is time-consuming, bitterly cold, and potentially dangerous.

Let's skip the debate over which came first, the lobster or the egg, and return to our lady lobster, who, for the convenience of this narrative, is still carrying her lover boy's sperm when she spawns, an event that occurs about once every two years. As she squirts out her eggs — ten thousand to one hundred thousand of them, depending on her age and size — she also fertilizes them by simultaneously releasing the sperm packets. Attaching the eggs to

Super Mom

A lobster "pregnancy" can last as long as two years. The female carries her mate's sperm for up to a year before releasing and, thus fertilizing, her eggs — ten thousand to one hundred thousand of them — which she then carries on her tail for another year.

the underside of her tail with a sticky substance produced by her swimmerets, she carries them for nine to twelve months while they develop. Should a Maine lobsterman catch her during this period, he cannot keep her. Instead, he must cut a small V-notch into her tail fin and throw her back into the sea, and as long as she bears that V-shaped scar, she cannot be sold, even if she is caught not bearing eggs. As a fertile female, she is worth more to the fishery alive and making babies than fetching a few bucks as someone's dinner.

NOAA

A "pregnant" lobster carries thousands of fertilized eggs, each one smaller than the head of a pin.

When the eggs hatch, the lobster releases them by fanning her swimmerets. The tiny flea-like larvae spend the next four to six weeks floating on the sea currents, shedding four times in the process. This is the most dangerous time of their lives, Cowan says, because "everything with a mouth big enough eats them." Only one-tenth of 1 percent of them survive to the fourth stage, when they look like miniature lobsters, each one smaller than your thumbnail. The small fry swim toward shore and dive to the ocean floor to find shelter under rocks and weeds.

In these lobster nurseries, which Cowan's Lobster Conservancy studies and seeks to protect, the lobsters live and grow. As they get bigger and bolder, they expand their range and move into deeper waters. It will be at least seven years before any of them reach the minimum legal size for market — 3 1/4 inches from the eyes to the beginning of the tail, about 1 pound. About that same time, the females reach sexual maturity. They get what Cowan calls PMS — pre-molt syndrome — when, like their mother before them, they tidy up their shelters and walk the watery streets in search of the toughest guy in the neighborhood. ✤

"...everything with a mouth big enough eats them."

The Lobster Conservancy Photo by Sara L. Ellis

The Lobster Conservancy Photo by John E. Cowan

with Lobster Scientist Diane Cowan

Of the dozen or so researchers who study lobsters in Maine, Diane Cowan follows the most unconventional path. By founding the Lobster Conservancy (TLC) in 1996, she has created a life that allows her to pursue her passion on her own terms. Her research lab is a six-acre lobster pound in Friendship, where she frequently dons scuba gear and spends hours watching and photographing its inhabitants. TLC engages dozens of residents in coastal communities from Massachusetts to Down East Maine in monitoring baby lobsters that can be found hiding under rocks on beaches during the lowest astronomical tides. Cowan and her volunteers spend several days each month, no matter the hour or the temperature, counting, measuring, and tagging the little crustaceans.

How did you become interested in lobster nurseries?

A I moved to Maine in August of 1992 to take a two-year teaching position at Bates College. After unpacking my boxes, my friend and I took a drive to the coast, and we ended up at Lowell Cove in Harpswell. There were two little boys on the shore, flipping rocks. We asked, "Hey, what are you guys doing?" They said, "We're playing with the baby lobsters." I was, like, "Whoa!" When I was in graduate school, the big question was, where do the little lobsters

"We're playing with the baby lobsters."

The Lobster Conservancy Photo by Diane F. Cowan

that start out as larvae in the open water, settle? It turns out the local people knew, but the scientists didn't.

Q **So you kept going back?**

 Yes. I involved my students at Bates in a research project counting lobsters. When that position ended, I couldn't go work for someone else because I couldn't leave my lobsters! So I moved to Harpswell and got a job at Cook's Lobster House. I gave them the tide schedule for the whole year and said, "These are the days I need off."

My first volunteers were the people of Harpswell — lobstermen, their wives, and kids, and the wait staff at Cook's. They learned how to measure lobsters, how to tell males from females, the differences between lobsters that are healthy and those that aren't. They learned how science looks at what they knew was there all the time. It is one thing to know the lobsters are there and another to take counts and have numbers that mean something.

"I couldn't leave my lobsters!"

My whole life changed. All my life's decisions are ruled by the tides, which is how I eventually ended up in Friendship. I've spent one week out of every month of my life with these babies for the past twenty years, and I am still amazed. I see something new every month.

The Lobster Conservancy Photo by Diane F. Cowan

Q **What do you hope to see happen as a result of your research?**

A We'd like to see the lobster nurseries protected at the town level. Harpswell has done some things — it adopted an ordinance preventing aerial spraying for pesticides around lobster nurseries. [Some insecticides inhibit the production of chitin, a major component of lobster shells.]

Q **How big are the lobsters that you find?**

A The smallest ones we find are three-quarters of an inch long. They're so adorable. They're unbelievably cute. I think that's why the volunteers do this.

Q **How do you put an identification tag on a lobster that small?**

A The tags are a little piece of wire, about one millimeter long and one-quarter millimeter in diameter. They look like a grain of sand. I have a hypodermic needle that has a plunger in it. I pick up the wire, put it in the needle, and then stick the tag into the lobster's foot — one of the legs behind the big claws that have the little pincers. The tag has a number on it that you can read under the microscope so you can tell who that lobster is. Of course, you have to get the tag back, so when I catch a lobster, I run it past a detector that beeps if there is a tag. I dissect the tag out, put it in a vial, then put a new tag in the lobster. The lobster never leaves the field. That's important, especially if you want to keep track of the same individual over time.

Q **What are some of the most surprising things you've learned?**

A Lobsters have this reputation as being solitary cannibals. That's because we usually encounter them in traps or tanks, and if you confine them, they do eat each other. But in nature, I've seen no evidence of this. In fact, the more I watch them, the more I am amazed at the complexity of their social structure and how they live together. I've found up to thirteen of my babies under one rock — usually they're the smaller ones who

Lobster Looms Large

The largest lobster ever caught weighed forty-four pounds, six ounces, and was between three and four feet long, according to the *Guinness Book of World Records*. It was caught off Nova Scotia in 1977. It was estimated to be one hundred years old. (The largest lobster in the scientific record was caught off Cape Cod in 1974 and weighed 42.5 pounds, according to Diane Cowan of the Lobster Conservancy.)

are less than a year old, the ones about three-quarters of an inch to an inch long. They are more likely to be with other lobsters than they are to be alone. The next bigger ones are found with other lobsters about half the time. Then as they get bigger, the more you are apt to find them alone.

I used to put lobsters in my pound, and they'd fight — they didn't want to be with each other. But now I just let them walk in and out when they want, so whoever is there wants to be there. There's typically one dominant male, a bunch of females, and a bunch of babies of different sizes, all living in incredibly high density, and they work out who's who, what's what, and they aren't killing each other.

> *"There's typically one dominant male..."*

Q **You seem to have a real affection for them.**

A I love them, and I know them as individuals. But I do eat lobsters — I just don't eat the individuals that I know! I buy my lobsters at the wharf from the lobstermen. Protect lobsters just for the sake of lobsters? No. The scientists and the fishermen want the same things: We want plenty of lobsters in our bellies tonight and plenty to catch tomorrow. ✤

Lobsters are delicious, but a meal also creates a lot of waste. Finding ways to make use of those empty red shells and picked carcasses is one of the tasks of the Lobster Institute, an organization whose broad mission is to conduct research and develop conservation practices and educational programs that will help sustain the lobster fishery in the United States and Canada.

Among the institute's inventions: biodegradable golf balls made from crushed lobster shells, a product that could well make hitting golf balls into the sea a favorite pastime of cruise ship passengers once again (the practice was ended in the 1980s when an international treaty banned the dumping of plastic at sea).

"We're really interested in byproducts," says Robert Bayer, the Lobster Institute's executive director

LOBSTER
...the Mother of Invention?

iStock Photo/
Joachim Anegltun

and a professor of veterinary and animal science at the University of Maine in Orono. "The whole concept that the meat industry follows is, 'Don't throw away anything.' We want to do that with the byproducts of lobster processing."

The results have included dog biscuits made from lobster meal (shells and residual meat) and a lobster shell plant pot, whose high calcium content benefits flowers and vegetables.

The idea for the lobster shell golf ball was first proposed by Carin Orr, one of Bayer's former graduate students. "So I played around with it," Bayer says. "I made the first ones in my basement." He then turned over the prototype — a crushed lobster shell core held together by a biodegadable glue and coating — to David Neivandt, an associate professor of biological and chemical engineering. Neivandt spent a year improving the design with the help of Alex Caddell,

Lobster processing creates a lot of waste, including shells, bodies, and residual meat. The Lobster Institute researches ways to use these byproducts.

Lobster shells are being used to make golf balls.

iStock Photo/Karen Locke

Photo courtesy of UMaine

a bioengineering major and a golfer. Their final product dissolves in the water in about three weeks. A private company is expected to market the golf balls in 2012.

Founded by the University and Maine lobster industry groups in the 1980s, the Lobster Institute has since broadened its reach to work with lobstermen and lobster industry representatives from Long Island Sound to Newfoundland. Its research, much of which is conducted by students and volunteers, encompasses virtually every aspect of the fishery. The institute has, for example, studied lobster shell disease, the effectiveness of the V-notch program, even the behavioral patterns of rare blue lobsters. It developed a test to detect "scrubbed" lobsters — lobsters whose eggs have been illegally removed by fishermen

Does your pup cast his sad, moist gaze on you whenever you eat lobster? No need to share your feast if you've got lobster meal biscuits, developed by the Lobster Institute, on hand.

Jennifer Anderson

— and it has experimented with alternative baits like cow-hide and soybeans (the industry is facing a shortage of herring, the bait traditionally used by lobstermen). The organization also is involved in policy and development, and it played a key role in the creation of the Maine Lobster Council, which markets and promotes Maine lobster around the world.

What next? "We're interested in finding ways to put shells into food products," Bayer says. "They are high in calcium and phosphorous, and studies suggest that could lower cholesterol. ❖

iStock Photo/Dianne Allen

Courtesy of the Lobster Institute

The Lobster Institute's research encompasses every aspect of the fishery.

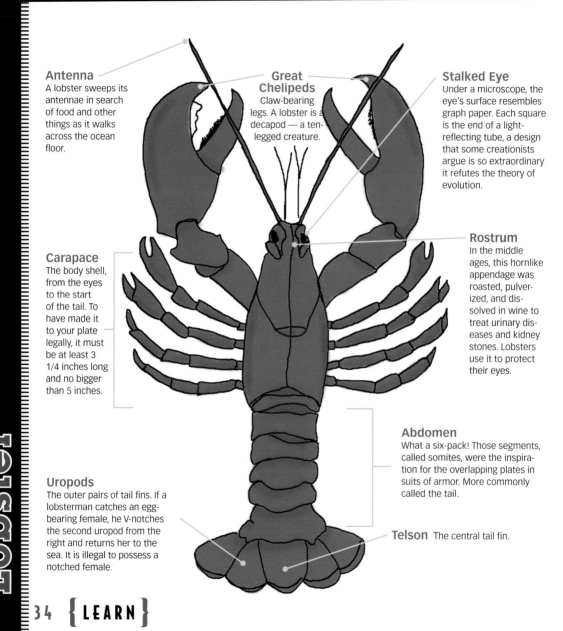

Antenna
A lobster sweeps its antennae in search of food and other things as it walks across the ocean floor.

Great Chelipeds
Claw-bearing legs. A lobster is a decapod — a ten-legged creature.

Stalked Eye
Under a microscope, the eye's surface resembles graph paper. Each square is the end of a light-reflecting tube, a design that some creationists argue is so extraordinary it refutes the theory of evolution.

Carapace
The body shell, from the eyes to the start of the tail. To have made it to your plate legally, it must be at least 3 1/4 inches long and no bigger than 5 inches.

Rostrum
In the middle ages, this hornlike appendage was roasted, pulverized, and dissolved in wine to treat urinary diseases and kidney stones. Lobsters use it to protect their eyes.

Abdomen
What a six-pack! Those segments, called somites, were the inspiration for the overlapping plates in suits of armor. More commonly called the tail.

Uropods
The outer pairs of tail fins. If a lobsterman catches an egg-bearing female, he V-notches the second uropod from the right and returns her to the sea. It is illegal to possess a notched female.

Telson The central tail fin.

Lobster

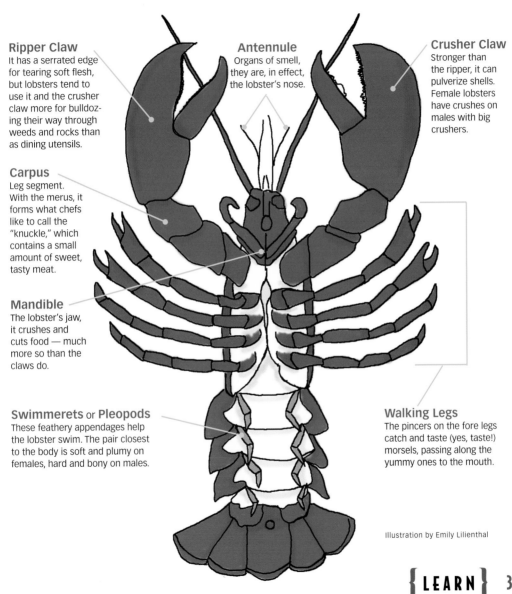

Ripper Claw
It has a serrated edge for tearing soft flesh, but lobsters tend to use it and the crusher claw more for bulldozing their way through weeds and rocks than as dining utensils.

Antennule
Organs of smell, they are, in effect, the lobster's nose.

Crusher Claw
Stronger than the ripper, it can pulverize shells. Female lobsters have crushes on males with big crushers.

Carpus
Leg segment. With the merus, it forms what chefs like to call the "knuckle," which contains a small amount of sweet, tasty meat.

Mandible
The lobster's jaw, it crushes and cuts food — much more so than the claws do.

Swimmerets or **Pleopods**
These feathery appendages help the lobster swim. The pair closest to the body is soft and plumy on females, hard and bony on males.

Walking Legs
The pincers on the fore legs catch and taste (yes, taste!) morsels, passing along the yummy ones to the mouth.

Illustration by Emily Lilienthal

QUIZ

Lobster Lingo

1 A berried lobster is:

A. A female carrying eggs under her tail

B. A lobster baked and stuffed with buttered breadcrumbs and wild blueberries. A Maine classic!

C. A lobster with a spotted shell. Also known as a calico lobster

2 What do you call a female lobster?

A. Jill

B. sow

C. hen

3 What do you call a male lobster?

A. Jack

B. boar

C. cock

4 A ghost trap is:

A. A lobster trap that is empty when pulled out of the ocean

B. A lobster trap that has come loose from its buoy but continues to capture lobsters

C. The contraption Bill Murray uses to catch ghosts in the movie *Ghostbusters*. It has nothing to do with lobsters

5 What do you call a lobster that has lost both claws?

A. pistol

B. bullet

C. dummie

6 An egger is:

A. An aggressive lobster, so called because it eggs other lobsters into fights

B. A female carrying eggs under her tail

C. A lobster omelet

7. A chicken lobster is:

A. A lobster that swims away from a fight with another lobster

B. Lobster meat coated with seasoned flour and pan-fried, a cooking method inspired by chicken-fried steak

C. A small lobster, typically weighing about one pound

8. A cull is:

A. A lobster that must be thrown back into the ocean because it is too small or too big for market

B. A lobster whose flaws make it unsuitable for sale live, therefore it is culled for processing and sold as parts

C. A lobster with only one claw

9. Tomalley is:

A. lobster roe

B. lobster liver

C. lobster brain

10. The bitter end is:

A. The inboard end of an anchor rope

B. The last lobster dinner of the season

C. A spoiled lobster tail

RED LOBSTER?

Most live lobsters are greenish black in color, though orange, yellow, white, and even brilliant blue lobsters have been caught. Lobsters turn red only when they are cooked. No wonder Mainers chuckled in 2009 over the name of their new NBA Development League team: the Red Claws.

Answers: 1-A; 2-C; 3-C; 4-B; 5-A, B & C; 6-B; 7-C; 8-C; 9-B; 10-A

Once in a
Blue Lobster

Blue lobsters have a genetic defect. Their shells do not contain all the pigments that lend normal lobsters greenish-brown color. Genetic defects also cause other unusual colorings, such as orange, yellow, and rarest of all, white.

Most American lobsters are greenish brown to dark bluish green, but every now and then a lobsterman finds something unusual in his trap — a bright blue lobster, maybe, or a lobster split perfectly down the middle by color, brown on one side, orange on the other. "Being a colored lobster may be appealing to us, but it makes the lobster genetically weaker and susceptible to heavier predation," says Aimee Hayden-Roderiques,

Courtesy of the Lobster Institute

Blue
1 in 2 million

Orange
1 in 10 million

Yellow
1 in 30 million

Calico
Mottled Orange and Black
1 in 30 million

Split
Half Orange-Half Brown
1 in 50 million

Albino
1 in 100 million

Source: The Lobster Institute and the
Maine State Aquarium

Maine State Aquarium Photos by Aimee Roderiques

manager of the Maine State Aquarium in Boothbay Harbor. "I have seen lobsters in almost every shade, including teal, purple, and pink. It's just a matter of genetic painting — how lobster DNA mixes and suppresses the codes for blue, red, and yellows that are responsible for the traditional brownish lobsters we see every day. One of the perks of working in the aquarium is getting these lobster surprises. We have had lobsters with all sorts of deformities, including several claws. We also get hermaphroditic lobsters, and once, and even rarer, a hermaphroditic split-colored lobster. My favorite to date? A teal and blue lobster with pink and purple claws. It molted and left out the pinks and purples, but changed into a really beautiful teal, green, and blue speckled lobster, like an Easter egg." ✤

Lobsters can lose claws, legs, eyes, and antennae in battle or an accident, but they are able to regenerate them. The lobster at left grew a few extra claws.

The Maine State Aquarium has extraordinary lobsters in many sizes and colors.

Maine Lobster
by the Numbers

14

Percentage a lobster's carapace increases in length after molting. The animal also experiences a 40 percent weight gain.

27 Number of times a lobster molts from the time it is a first-stage larva to the time it reaches legal minimum size harvesting (a seven- to nine-year time span)

1
PERCENTAGE OF EGGS that survive to adult size.

30 **Minutes** it takes for a lobster to molt.

21.9 million
Pounds of lobster harvested in Maine in 1980.

103 million
Pounds of lobster landed in Maine in 2011, a new record.

iStock Photo/ Sawayasu Tsuji

10,000 – 100,000
Number of eggs produced by an adult female lobster. The older she is, the more eggs she produces.

4,500 Number of lobstermen actively harvesting in Maine.

800
Maximum number of traps a Maine lobsterman may set.

©jesse welter — Fotolia.com

$7.95
Typical retail price for a one-pound lobster in Maine in December 2011. Prices fluctuate with the seasons (soft-shell lobsters, usually available in late summer, are less expensive than hard shell) and demand.

iStock Photo/Luis Albuquerque

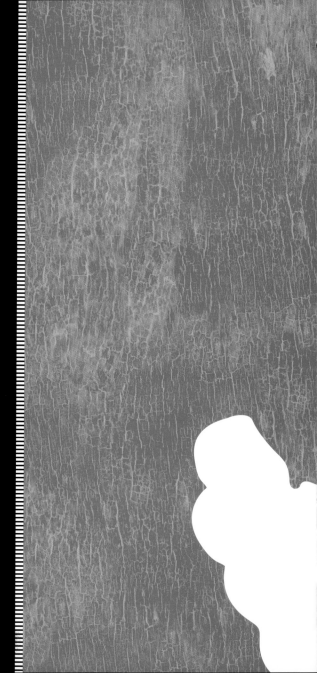

Lobsters and lobster-ing are a way of life in coastal Maine, from the men and women who haul in the 100 million pounds of lobster each year to the hordes of tourists who line up at our seafood shacks for lobster rolls. And we celebrate our ubiq-uitous crustacean in every way imagin-able, from festivals to souvenirs.

Lobstering colors life all along Maine's three thousand-mile coastline, and many villages have developed peculiar traditions around this culture. Here is a glimpse at a few of them.

Lobster Towns

iStock Photo/Veronica Munsey

Rockland is the self-proclaimed Lobster Capital of the World, but does it have the credentials to support that claim? That depends. The city is home to the Maine Lobster Festival, the state's oldest and biggest lobster celebration, drawing one hundred thousand people who gobble up more than twenty thousand pounds of lobster over five days every summer. But when it comes to the size and value of the catch, Rockland is not the leading port it once was. In fact, it was number twelve in 2010, with

dealers reporting landings of 2,118,440 pounds, valued at $7,551,932.

Stonington has emerged as the new center of lobster abundance in Maine. Since 2008, the port has led the state in lobster landings. In 2010, Stonington lobstermen brought in 13,786,249 pounds of lobster, valued at $44,262,500.

Matinicus Island, located twenty miles off the coast of Rockland, is infamous as an example of lobstering's territorial culture. In truth, lobstermen from Saco to Stonington have waged feuds in recent years, with fishermen cutting each other's trap lines and even sinking a few boats. But it is also true that the lobster wars have been especially ugly on Matincus. In 2009, one fisherman shot and wounded another, the culmination of a dispute over fishing rights that had been escalating for months.

Pat and Chuck Blackley

Monhegan Island Monhegan has its own state-sanctioned fishing zone, the Monhegan Lobster Conservation Area, where only island fishermen can set traps. The island fleet fishes only in the winter, when most other ports are all but closed down. That's because lobster populations around the island are at their highest in winter when the crustaceans migrate to the warmer, deep waters offshore. The season is launched with Trap Day on October 1, when the entire community rises before dawn to help the lobstermen carry their traps to the dock and their waiting boats.

Pat and Chuck Blackley

LIVE

Jonesport and Beals Island, neighboring towns way Down East in Washington County, lay claim to the tallest Christmas tree fashioned from lobster traps. Lobstermen in the community built their first trap tree in 2010. At fifty-two feet, it upstaged both Rockland and the Massachusetts port of Gloucester, who have engaged in a spirited battle to build the biggest and best trap tree for several years. In 2011, the Jonesport-Beals tree grew to sixty feet. It was topped by a cross made from buoys that belonged to Jacob Beal, a fisherman who had died in a recreational boating accident.

Cara Fealy Choate

Gouldsboro illustrates the shift in Maine's fishing trends in an unusual way. There, on the shores of Prospect Harbor, you'll find Big Jim, a thirty-foot-tall fisherman holding a lobster trap. The trap is the old-fashioned wooden variety, but it is a relatively new possession for Jim, who spent most of his life holding an oversized sardine can. Sardines were once Maine's largest industry, peaking in the 1950s with forty-six canneries scattered along the coast, and Big Jim, initially

Nance Trueworthy

installed on Route 1 in Kittery, was the Maine Sardine Council's way of trumpeting that fact. In the 1960s, Stinson Seafood purchased the sign and erected it next to its Prospect Harbor sardine cannery. It processed its last sardine in April 2010. Big Jim traded his sardine can for a lobster trap when Live Lobster began processing lobster in the plant the following year. ❖

The Legend of the Lobster

By Sandra L. Oliver

If you believe everything you read or hear about lobsters, then you know that they used to be so plentiful that apprentices, prisoners, poorhouse occupants, boarders, and many other benighted souls refused to eat lobster more than twice a week. You know that farmers used lobsters for fertilizer,

plowing them into their fields. You've heard that once upon a time, anyone could wade into shore waters and gather up as many lobsters as they might want to eat. You know that children were embarrassed to take lobster sandwiches to school in their lunchboxes. You've read that Pilgrim governor Winthrop actually apologized for having only lobster to offer newcomers to Plymouth in 1622.

These stories are often retold, appear frequently in print, and are so persistent that they have acquired the aura of unassailable fact. Lots of really smart people have accepted the stories unquestioningly, and they are appealing tales. These "facts" are, however, either untrue or skewed enough to miss veracity's mark.

In 1622, Plymouth Colony's Governor William Bradford did say that all the colonists "could presente their friends with was a lobster ... without bread or anything else but a cupp of fair water." It wasn't a slam against lob-

Maine Maritime Museum

ster. It was a mere statement of fact: the colonists were subsisting on food they could gather to stave off hunger while they established gardens and farms to produce enough grain, meat, and vegetables to rely on. They would much rather have had beef, wheat bread, and beer, all of which packed the caloric punch these hard-working folks needed to power their clearing, building, and planting.

For a while in some places, lobster was plentiful enough that even youngsters could go-a-wading and pluck up a few to cook at the shore as a picnic snack. Maine coast fisherman Charlie York, growing up on Bailey Island in the early 1900s, recalled that as a boy he and his pals snagged lobsters and cooked them up in a pot by the shore to eat just for fun.

Lobsters did not stay that plentiful anywhere, however, because they were valued as food. The longer a coastal area was settled, the sooner it ran out of easy-to-find lobster. There was a market for lobster in New York by the 1740s where they were sold live from floating crates. In Boston they were caught, brought ashore, cooked, and then peddled to cooks who used them in sauces and pies.

Lobster was so plentiful, youngsters could go-a-wading and pluck a few for a picnic snack.

By the 1840s, Maine fishermen could sell lobster to visiting well-smacks — vessels with seawater flowing through a portion of the hull to carry the lobsters alive — that conveyed the shellfish back to Boston. As long as there was a market for lobster, the shellfish had value and sometimes was too valuable for the fisherman to eat. When the fisherman could not sell it, then it became subsistence fare, and, like the Plymouth colonists, most twentieth-century families preferred to eat meat, like beef or pork, rather than lobster. According to an old-timer neighbor of mine, a purchased hot dog had more appeal than seafood and showed that a family had cash, a situation economically preferable to sending the kids to school with lobster sandwiches.

One way of creating a reliable market for lobster was to develop canneries near the source. In Maine and elsewhere in New England by the later 1800s, dozens of small shoreside canneries boiled and packed easy-to-use lobster ready at a moment's notice for lobster salad or stew, relieving the cook of boiling whole, thrashing lobsters, then picking out the meat and tossing the shell mess. The canneries produced tons of cracked claws and carapaces, which neighboring farmers welcomed as organic material to add to their fields. City slickers, increasingly numerous along the Maine coast in the late 1800s and early 1900s, no doubt noticed red bits of boiled lobster shell plowed into the ground, and concluded that lobster must be so plentiful that farmers used them for fertilizer. They failed to notice the cannery whence came cans of luxurious lobster meat.

Most early twentieth-century families preferred a meal of pork or beef to lobster.

Lobster is a well-managed, productive fishery and with improved transcontinental — indeed, worldwide — distribution its value increased until in the twentieth century lobster was generally recognized in urban settings as a luxury seafood. So, as with other costly and relatively scarce resources, lobster took its place among high-value fare, setting it up for mythologizing about an earlier golden age of lobster-plenty-for-all. The stories about the town poor, prisoners, apprentices, and others rejecting over-abundant lobster, however, are all stories set in an earlier time before lobster moved from merely valuable to a luxury item. The real giveaway that this particular rendition of lobster lore is truly fake, is that the very same stories were told in the late 1800s about salmon, and they weren't true about salmon, either.

A typical example comes from Islesboro, Maine, and John P. Farrow's *History of Islesborough* published in 1893: "Tradition informs us that the salmon were so plenty (sic) that the first town poor protested against being served with salmon more than twice a week." The same tale is told about Lowell factory workers, lumbermen in the Northwest, apprentices in Boston — the list goes on and on. There is never any proof cited: the story always comes with the phrase "tradition has it" or "it is often said" or some similar vague attribution.

Stanley Museum

The stories are almost always told in the context of a time past when salmon were exceedingly plentiful and are often included in town or popular histories written in the late 1800s just as salmon stocks began to decline. Sometime in the early 1900s, the main character shifts from salmon to lobster, but other details do not change.

It is beguiling to imagine a time when lobster was freely plentiful, when anyone could eat it, and we marvel at why anyone would turn down such luxury fare. Surely we'd not miss such a chance. Perhaps someday the story will be told about beef tenderloin. ❖

Sandra L. Oliver is a food historian and the author of Maine Home Cooking *and other cookbooks. She lives on the island of Islesboro.*

A lobster pound is a live storage facility traditionally located in a deep tidal creek or harbor, where fresh seawater flows in and out. The term "lobster pound" also is sometimes used interchangeably with lobster shack.

Maine State Archive

LOBSTER ICE CREAM

A smiling lobster welcomes ice cream lovers to Ben & Bill's.

Think of it as frozen lobster bisque. The lobster ice cream at Ben & Bill's Chocolate Emporium on Main Street in Bar Harbor has been eliciting double-takes ever since owner Bill Coggins introduced it in the 1990s. "A couple told him that they loved the store's selection of chocolates and ice cream, but they wished that it had something with lobster in it," says manager Roy Gott. "Bill told them to come back in a few days and he'd have something for them."

A butter-based vanilla ice cream studded with butter-marinated lobster chunks, the confection is not as popular as conventional flavors like mint chip and chocolate, Gott says, but it sells surprisingly well. A spoonful starts out tasting like rich vanilla ice cream, and the lobster flavor kicks in as the seafood thaws. "People come in and they are very skeptical," Gott says. "But then they try it and most say it's nothing like what they expected. I've only seen two people spit it out." ❖

Maine's first graphic license plate, introduced in 1987, sported the image of a red lobster and was designed by elementary school children. Critics said the image was so small that it looked more like a bug than a lobster. It was replaced by a chickadee plate in 2000. A new lobster plate, this time with a cooked crustacean on a rock and a fisherman's shed in the background, was issued in 2003.

Ben & Bill's Emporium/Roy Gott

Bill Coggins invented lobster ice cream, a butter-based vanilla ice cream studded with chunks of lobster. Here it's being served with a chocolate-dipped waffle cone.

Lobsterman Ty Babb's workday begins before sunrise, when he drives from his home in Martinsville to nearby Tenants Harbor, picking up his sternman, Paul Estes, along the way. On the dock, the men load barrels of ripe-smelling bait — usually salted herring — onto the deck of Babb's boat, the *Haley's Comet.* By the time the sun is rising over the horizon, they are motoring out to Babb's first fluorescent yellow buoy, which is tethered to a cage-wire trap that is weighted and resting on the ocean floor.

Portrait
of a
Lobsterman

Nance Trueworthy

Working near the bow, Babb snags the buoy with a gaff, a long pole with a hooked end. He loops the line onto the block, a mechanical winch that pulls the trap out of the sea. Guiding the dangling trap onto the lobster-boat's wide gunnel, Babb gets his first close look at what's inside. "I like it when it comes up and it's full," he says, a twinkle in his eye.

The son of a lobsterman, Babb has been fishing for lobsters since he was six years old, when he had one trap. When he was a teenager, he was taught how

There's a skill to setting lobster traps, Ty Babb says: "It's like pole fishing, but you've got to remember how you made your cast three days ago."

Each lobsterman "brands" his buoys with a unique color scheme, which helps him identify his traps. Once made of wood, buoys are now made of Styrofoam.

to build his own traps by the late Sherwood Cook, who was known around Tenants Harbor as much for his bird carvings and knowledge of Maine history as he was for his lobstering prowess. Babb recalls proudly showing Cook how well he'd tied the funnel-shaped mesh entrances on his first trap. "That's pretty good," Cook said. Then with a penknife, he cut each of the strings that held the netting taut. "Tomorrow you'll do it better."

There's a skill to tying those tunnels of netting so lobsters can get in and not get out, Babb learned that day, and he's learned since that there is a skill to setting the traps so they sit flat on the ocean floor, rather than getting hung up on a rock. "Anyone can catch a lobster near that rock if they haul at low tide and they can see it," he says. "But if it's high tide, you have to imagine where it is. And if the tide was cranky, if it was a little rough, it would be harder to guess where that trap is going to land. It's like pole fishing, but you've got to remember how you made your cast three days ago."

Babb fishes with eight hundred traps, the maximum allowed in the Gulf of Maine. When he worked out of Islesboro, an island three miles off Lincolnville Beach, he fished pairs — two traps per buoy — but here, inside Muscle Ridge Channel, the custom is one buoy, one trap. Some years he fishes into the winter,

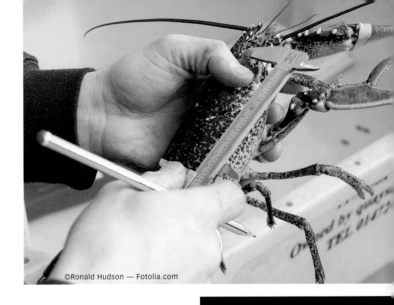

©Ronald Hudson — Fotolia.com

which means following the lobsters to deeper waters and setting his traps fifteen miles offshore. He checks each trap every three days.

Babb always lands the first trap. "It makes [Paul] appreciate me more," he says wryly. He cleans out everything inside, throwing crabs and other fish overboard and tossing the lobsters onto a sorting table where he measures each crustacean, ensuring the carapace is between 3.25 and 5 inches long, and bands its claws before putting it into a holding tank. If the lobster is too short or too big, it goes overboard, as does any egg-bearing female once Babb has notched a V into her tail, a signal to any other

Maine lobstermen measure each lobster from eye socket to the back of the carapace to ensure that it is legal size: at least 3 1/4 inches and no more than 5 inches. Anything smaller or bigger must be thrown back in the sea.

Babb has caught
blue lobsters but
resisted keeping
them as trophies.

fisherman who catch her that she is a fertile female and cannot be kept. He finds five to ten "eggers" in every fifteen traps.

"The size limits and the V-notch law are what make our fishery," Babb says. "Notching the females is a big deal. There is a lot of luck to lobstering, but it can't be bad luck to throw over a nice berried female."

He has caught rare blue, speckled, and white lobsters and resisted the temptation to take them home and keep them in his freezer as conversation pieces. "They're magnificent," he says, "but if you took them home they would be disappointing pretty quick because when they're dead, they're dead."

While Babb sorts the catch, Estes re-baits the trap and drops it back into the sea. Within minutes, they are puttering to the next buoy. By day's end, Babb and Estes will deliver the contents of some two hundred to three hundred traps to a dealer's truck waiting in Tenants Harbor or Port Clyde.

"People say lobstering is a short season, but if you leave at 4 a.m. and come home at 7 p.m., it's not too short," Babb says. Not that he's complaining. "I think it's great. I get to shirk off and go fishing six days a week." ❖

Maine Catch!

Maine's annual lobster catch is valued at over $300 million, comprising about 70 percent of the state's seafood harvest.

Nance Trueworthy

AFTER THE HARVEST

Many lobstermen sell their catch to dealers and processors who have lobster pounds and processing facilities on the water. Among these is Atlantic Edge Lobster, which buys from roughly twenty lobsterboats that deliver right to its dock on Boothbay Harbor.

One wall of the Atlantic Edge facility, which is not much bigger than a four-car garage, is lined with shallow green tanks, where hundreds of lobsters crawl about until they are trucked to Cozy Harbor Seafood in Portland, one of Maine's largest seafood dealers and processors. From there, the lobsters may be sold live or cooked and frozen

to supermarkets, wholesalers, and restaurants throughout the United States, Canada, and parts of Europe. A portion of Atlantic Edge's lobsters — usually those with the softest shells because they don't travel well — is cooked on site in an industrial-size pot of boiling water in a small room at the rear of the building. The hot lobsters are then deposited on a table, and the company's single full-time picker snaps off tails and gently cracks the claws to extract the meat within. The cooked meat is sold to area restaurants, such as Red's Eats in Wiscasset, which stuffs it into its famous lobster rolls. ❖

Lobster Legs
Spaghetti

iStock Photo/Elena
Zapassky/Ivan Mateev

We've been eating lobster all our lives, but we didn't know that a lobster's fantail contains meat until we paid a visit to Shucks in Richmond, Maine. Even if we had known, it would have made little difference; we couldn't possibly have picked a morsel from that paper-thin shell.

The shuckers at Shucks can. Not only that, they can extract that exquisitely delicate, blossom-shaped meat without separating it from the chewier tail. And the meat is raw to boot. The "Big Mother Shucker," a two-story, eighty thousand-pound machine that uses high water pressure to instantly kill lobsters and loosen their uncooked meat from their shells, makes it possible.

"When people eat lobster, they want food, not an animal," believes Shucks CEO John Hathaway. "Lobster is one of the last animals that people have to buy and kill to turn into food themselves."

Hathaway speaks from his experience as the owner of a Kennebunkport lobster shack. "I'm no chef, but I can boil water, so I figured I could sell lobster dinners, cold beer, and drinks, and everyone would be happy," he says. "I quickly came to the realization that that's not what people wanted. I was shocked, actually. Instead, anything we put lobster meat on, rolls, salads, pasta, sold well. And if they did order the lobster dinner, which they didn't do very often, then they wanted me to cut it and make it a lazy man's lobster. It opened my eyes to what people wanted — especially people who aren't from Maine."

Then Hathaway heard about a Louisiana oysterman whose experiments with high-pressure processing to kill off bacteria and parasites in raw oysters produced a side benefit: the process shucked the oyster as well. Hathaway paid a visit to the oysterman, who obliged his request

Shucks Maine Lobster/
Suellen Hathaway

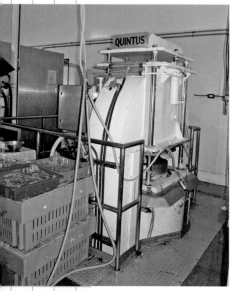

to put lobsters in the processing machine and, lo, it shucked lobsters, too. In fact, it did it far more cleanly than boiling or steaming: Knuckles, those little joints that confound even the most experienced pickers, gave up their meat still attached to the claws. Legs slipped out of their shells whole, looking like fat, pink spaghetti noodles. And that fantail meat emerged intact, too.

With a high-pressure processor that he found in Australia, Hathaway opened Shucks in a former golf shoe factory in 2005. There, in a large cement-floored room, dozens of people in white lab coats and purple aprons work steadily at stainless-steel tables, cracking lobster shells with their hands and nudging out the raw meat. Others sort shucked meat into packages, which then ride a conveyer belt through a freezer tunnel. In a back corner, a man feeds a metal basket filled with two hundred pounds of live lobsters into an opening in the tank-like Big Mother Shucker (a.k.a. the Avure 215L). The basket sinks into a water-filled chamber, where a pump pressurizes the water to fifty thousand pounds per square inch — "way more than the deepest point of the ocean," Hathaway says — killing the lobsters (and the bacteria that

would make their meat spoil) in just six seconds and disconnecting their flesh from the exoskeleton. When the lobsters emerge six minutes later, their shells are still the greenish black color of live lobsters, but they are no longer moving. The basket's contents is then distributed amongst the shucking crews, who handle roughly ten thousand pounds of lobster every day.

Shucks is the only company in the United States that uses extreme water pressure to shuck lobsters, but it's that raw meat that really sets it apart. Shipping frozen raw meat is far less complicated than shipping live lobsters, and Shucks is selling its products — including lobster leg spaghetti — to markets in Europe and Asia (the company won the Best Service Product and another for Best Convenience Product awards at the 2007 European Seafood Exposition in Belgium).

In the kitchen, where it really counts, raw lobster meat is allowing chefs to be more creative. "Before this, chefs had to either buy cooked meat or they could blanch a live lobster and extract the meat themselves," Hathaway says. "Either way, they were working with cooked meat, and when you recook lobster meat, it loses some of its magic — it becomes chewy. It's as if you bought cooked steak and reheated it." ❖

Shari Ciomei

with Lobsterman Julie Eaton

The cover girl on the 2012 *Lobsterwomen of Maine* calendar, Julie Eaton, who prefers to be called a lobsterman, fishes out of Stonington aboard the thirty-foot *Cat Sass.* Because the boat is small and narrow, Eaton typically works without a sternman and sets four hundred traps, half the legal limit. Every July she races *Cat Sass* in the Stonington Lobsterboat Races, regularly placing among the top three finishers in the smallest diesel class.

Q You came to lobstering by way of a circuitous path that began after you were seriously hurt in a car accident. Explain what happened.

A That was in 1987, four days after my twenty-third birthday. I had been to college in Salt Lake City, where I majored in aeronautical science. I got my commercial pilot's license while I was out there. When I came home to Surry, I wanted to do something that would benefit people, so I applied to the Maine State Police, with the idea of becoming a rescue pilot.

Then I had the car accident. My whole world changed. I was in a coma for a long time. When I came out of it, I was in the fetal position. In all ways, I had reverted back to being an infant. They had to teach me to talk and walk and read and write all over again.

Q How long did it take you to recover?

A I had intensive therapy for three years — every day, all day, just like going to school. Now, the biggest problem that remains is my memory. I couldn't tell you what I had for breakfast this morning. Things like starting the boat engine have to be routine, the same every time.

Traditionally, a lobsterman names his boat after his mother and daughter, hence all those fishing vessels with two female names. Traditions are meant to be broken, however, and many fishermen express themselves with their boat names. Julie Eaton named her boat *Cat Sass* because of the way it sounds when you say it fast.

If it's routine, I can just get on the boat and do it. But if something different happens, like my boat springs a leak, I make the call on the VHF radio: "I've got trouble."

 When did you start fishing?

 While I was recovering, I made friends with a fisherman, Bud Kilton from Sorrento — actually, I knew him before the accident, but I didn't remember him. He took divers out scalloping and he let me come along because he thought it would be good for me. I had the mental ability of a three-year-old, and it was very healing, very calming. I'd run around with a towel drying the divers' faces when they came out of the water. I thought I was being a help, but I was being a real pain in the ass. Those guys were very tolerant. That summer I got certified as a diver, and I scalloped for several years. Then I decided I needed to work year-round, so I moved to Vinalhaven and became a lobsterman.

Was it hard to break in there?

It was an honor to be able to fish on Vinalhaven. I had no birthright to be there. But the guys found a little soft spot for me. They took me under their wings and taught me the ropes. I sterned for different people, and then I got my little outboard.

Q **Why did you leave Vinalhaven?**

A The boathouse I was living in was sold, so I moved off island and rented a place in Penobscot. It was like starting all over again because this wasn't my territory. I worked at the Stonington Lobster Co-op for a while, then I got a sterning spot with one of the guys. While I was working for him, I met the man I had followed in the lobsterboat races forever, Sidney Eaton. He is quite famous in my line of work — he has had the fastest lobsterboat title more times than anybody. He was my hero. I wanted to be just like him.

The first lobster pound was built on Vinalhaven island in 1875.

Maine Historic Preservation commission

Q **Sidney Eaton — the man who would become your husband!**

A He was married when I met him. In fact, I was good friends with his wife — she had visited me on Vinalhaven many times. I always say that when she passed away from cancer, she left Sidney to me in her will.

Several months after she died, I called Sidney to ask if I could run his boat in the ladies' lobsterboat race. He said, "Yes, but you're going to have to practice because it's very powerful." We met, and I got to drive his boat for the first time — it took off so fast, it set me right on my butt! I raced her the next day and I won all the big prizes.

 And the rest is history...

 We dated for a week, and when my landlord took the roof off my house to add a second story, Sidney said, "Get your bag and come on down." So after a week of dating, we moved in together. After a month of living together, we got engaged. And after eleven months of being engaged, we got married. He is in every way my Superman.

You and Sidney each have your own boat, but you also work together.

That's right. I could fish eight hundred traps, and he could fish eight hundred traps, but instead we do four hundred apiece. That way, when we're setting out in spring or taking up in fall, we can do it together legally in his boat, which is much faster than mine.

So you don't fish in winter?

A Not in my boat. I sign on with another boat as a third man because I just can't give it up. When we take my boat out in the fall, I get teary. Sidney, who has fished for fifty-eight years, is ready to come in because everything is different in winter.

How so?

A We fish offshore, and you get out there in a twenty-foot rolling swell and the boat is turning all the time. You're as green as the green water is. I get seasick every day, but I don't care because I'm out there. I went to donate blood a few weeks ago, and they wouldn't take it — they said I had saltwater in my veins. I'm just part of the ocean now. It's what I eat. It's what I sleep. It's who I am. ❖

Entrance Head or Funnel.
Lobsters enter through this mesh tunnel, which narrows toward the trap's interior, making it difficult for them to back out.

Escape Vent or Ghost Panel.
These hatches are designed to biodegrade and release lobsters should the trap be lost at sea.

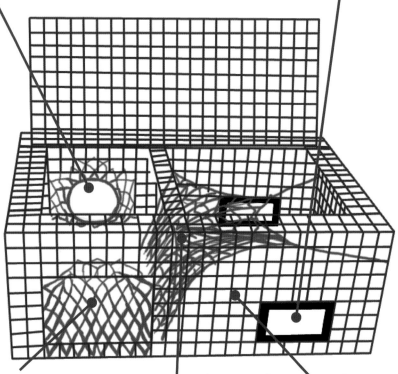

Kitchen. Here's where the bait, usually salted herring, awaits the lobsters. Because they cannot easily exit the way they came, satiated lobsters typically crawl into the . . .

Parlor Head or Funnel, which leads to the . . .

Parlor. Theoretically, there is no way out of the parlor, but University of New Hampshire zoologist Win Watson's underwater video (see page 17) suggests lobsters are not so easily trapped.

Illustration by Emily Lilienthal

A lobster tattoo may symbolize strength, abundance, and surely, good taste!

Nance Trueworthy

Shannon Kinney

The fire trucks line up on Broadway. The Sea Princesses gather on Main. The politicians huddle on Birch. Scattered up and down these and other nearby side streets are seventy or so idling flatbed trailers, atop of which sit mermaids, pirates, sea captains, and countless people dressed in red tee shirts, red pants, and red hats sprouting claws like antlers. "It's organized chaos," says Jen Chapman, manager of the Big Parade, a cornerstone of the Maine Lobster Festival, a loud, steamy, jubilant affair that draws nearly one hundred thousand people to the midcoast city of Rockland every August. "And it's the coolest thing I've ever been involved with."

It is Chapman who gives the word — always at 10 a.m. on Saturday, the festival's busiest day — that starts all those disparate parts moving into place, one behind the other, then rolling,

LOBSTER
Festivities

marching, dancing, and prancing through downtown Rockland. Always leading the parade are two hundred sailors from whichever ship the navy has sent to pay a port visit, and always bringing up the rear some ninety minutes later is a seven hundred-pound bright red lobster named Rocky. Most everything in between is designed to reflect the festival's theme, which more often than not involves lobsters (some examples: "Lighthouses, Laughter and Lobster," "From the Ocean to the Table," and "Lobster-Palooza").

For most of the attendees, the Lobster Festival is a brief highlight of summer, but for the thirty-five volunteers who organize it, it is a yearlong effort, says Alice Knight, who attended the first Lobster Festival in 1947, when she was thirteen, and has been involved in planning it since the early 1970s. A small, relatively simple celebration until

A seven hundred pound lobster named Rocky always brings up the rear of the Maine Lobster Festival parade.

Three images here courtesy Maine Lobster Festival. Photos by Michael Whitman

People from all over the country plan their vacations around the Maine Lobster Festival, which features big-name entertainers and, of course, lots of lobster.

the 1990s, the festival was transformed into one of the Northeast's top summer attractions when organizers began booking big-name entertainers like Willie Nelson and Lee Ann Womack. "These days, people from all over the country plan their vacations around it," Knight says.

They come for the concerts in Rockland's Harbor Park and to partake in lobster-themed events like the Great International William Atwood Lobster Crate Race, in which contestants trot across a string of fifty partially submerged lobster crates (the winner is the person who runs the most

The Lobster Festival is lobster dinners and lobster crate races ...

Three images here courtesy Maine Lobster Festival. Photos by Michael Whitman

crates before falling into ocean). They also come to feast, consuming more than twenty thousand pounds of lobster at the festival every year. "They're always happy," Knight says. "People are always happy when they're eating lobster." ❖

...and big name entertainers and carnival rides.

Becca Gildred

Courtesy Maine Lobster Festival.
Photo by Michael Whitman

with Maine Sea Goddess Kristen Sawyer

Three months after she graduated from Georges Valley High
School in Thomaston, Kristen Sawyer was crowned Maine
Sea Goddess at the sixty-fourth annual Maine Lobster Festival in August of 2011. She grew up on the St. George pen-
insula and spent her summers working at Miller's Lobster
Co., a lobster shack and pound on the wharf in the fishing
village of Spruce Head. Sawyer is majoring in social work

at Gordon College in Wenham, Massachusetts. After she graduates, she plans to return to midcoast Maine to pursue a career as a high-school guidance counselor. As the Maine Sea Goddess, her duties are to represent the lobster industry at events around New England for one year.

Q. Why did you want to be the Maine Sea Goddess?

A. I wanted to show my love and appreciation for the place where I grew up. Whenever I needed a break or wanted to get away, all I had to do was walk up the street and down a little path and I'd be on my own private little beach. It's hard to put into words how incredible it is to grow up close to the ocean. There's nothing else on earth that is so immense and powerful. The sea gives our community life.

Q. Are you from a fishing family?

A. No, but my father is a pastor and our congregation is full of fishermen. My mother works as a certified public accountant from our home, and her clients are lobstermen, bait companies, and trap mills. Everyone is working together for a similar purpose, so the community is very close knit.

A It's a small lobster shack right on the wharf, with picnic tables on one side and the guys bringing in the catch on the other. We meet them and put the lobsters in tanks. There are usually four or five of us working, plus the owners, Gail and Mark Miller. We split up the tasks between us — one cook, one lobster-roll maker, one window person, and one or two waitresses preparing trays and carrying them out. And we all answer a lot of questions from the customers.

Q Like what?

A The most common question is, what is the difference between a hard shell and a soft shell lobster? We offer both, and they want us to explain the price difference. Often customers ask for the biggest lobster we have — a two-pounder, which is big and old. It probably has some scars and dings and it's not as smoothly red as the smaller lobsters. The customers will come up to the window and ask, "What did you do to this lobster? You burned it!"

A It was a long process. There were eighteen of us. We applied in April and learned that we were in the program in mid-May. We participated in a number of events over the summer, including a train ride to Brunswick, where my group toured the Maine State Music Theatre. We also had princess practices, where we would rehearse the things we need to know for the coronation, like how to walk on the stage and answer interview questions. When we got closer to the coronation, we attended a banquet with people from the community. We were called up to the podium one by one and asked questions about our aspirations and our knowledge of the midcoast, lobstering, and the festival's history.

Q **It sounds intimidating.**

A It was a little, but at the same time, I viewed it as a learning experience. The judges were warm and open and made an effort to get to know us on a personal level. They provided a good support system; you could ask them about anything.

They began the day I was crowned. I walked around the festival greeting people and having my picture taken with them. I'm such a people person that I loved every moment of it. People had come from all over the country — they planned their vacation around the Lobster Festival. Growing up, we used to complain about the tourists and the traffic they caused, but I understand better now that tourism is an important industry in Maine. It holds us up.

Courtesy Maine Lobster Festival.
Photo by Michael Whitman

Since then I've represented Maine at a lot of festivals and fairs, including the Big E in Springfield, Massachusetts, where I met Governor Paul LePage.

Have you ever been lobstering?

Once. I was dating a lobsterman and I fell into the tray of bait!

Do you like lobster?

Oh my gosh, I love lobster! ❖

Lobster

By Ben W. Smith

On one particularly hazy and head-pounding Sunday morning in LA, coffee alone would not do. A hike in Griffith Park would not sweat this one out. Even the comparably fresh air of Manhattan Beach couldn't expel this feeling. This East Coast transplant needed something different. Something primal. I needed the odor of the Atlantic. I needed the slap in the face of cold Maine air. I needed home.

I needed lobster.

Port of Los Angeles Lobster Festival

Ben W. Smith

As it happened, the largest lobster festival in the world, the Port of Los Angeles Lobster Festival, was in full swing. It wasn't Maine, but it was something. There had to be a reason the Maine Lobster Council would approve it as a Maine Lobster Festival, right? So I threw on baggy jeans, old running shoes, my Ricetta's Pizzeria T-shirt, and a Red Sox cap, and my roommate and I made our way down from Silver Lake to San Pedro, a couple of Atlantic coast natives looking for a little solace in a big Pacific city.

"Indeed, this is large," I thought as I entered through the archway made from giant inflatable lobster claws. Forty thousand West Coasters attended the festival. While impressive, bigness was not precisely what I was seeking — I wanted authenticity. We waded in among the vendor booths, mostly clothing, jewelry, car and vacation contests — most with no relevance at all to Maine or lobster for that matter. There was one Maine vendor at the festival,

Obsidian Productions

lobstertank.com, a lobster shipping business out of Casco Bay. A much smaller operation, seemingly geared at private consumption, than Spruce Head's William Atwood Lobster Company, which

All photos this page, Ben W. Smith

supplied the festival's 32,000 lobsters, 30,000 of which were sold. The festival's organizer, Jim Hall, a Californian inspired by the Maine Lobster Festival in Rockland, did not dignify my request for the two thousand leftovers with a response.

We ventured deeper into the festival, encountering actors dressed up as pirates, live music, a wood-fired pizza truck, and attendees with fuzzy lobster claw hats. I became increasingly concerned I would not get my Maine fix. Then we made our way to the lobster tent. There, an army of women prepped the lobsters for us by hacking at the shells with knives, making crackers (metal, not edible) unnecessary. Harry chose the full meal, which included a roll, home-fry-style potatoes, and something the festival's Web site calls "buttery dippin' sauce." I figured corn was a more authentic pairing, so I got myself a single lobster and corn on the cob from a separate vendor. We carried our trays to a standing table and tore in. I abstained from the dippin' sauce to no ill-effect; the lobster was plenty salty, buttery, and delicious all on its own. A wave of contentment washed over me. Sure, I prefer to crack into the lobster's shell myself, but pulling it apart with my bare hands was gratifying in itself. Indeed, the Port of Los Angeles Lobster Festival had managed to ship me a little Maine comfort three thousand miles from home. ❖

Ben W. Smith has relocated to Brooklyn, where he works as a writer and filmmaker.

Undoubtedly, the best part about Maine lobster is eating it. A quick primer: Lobsters are cooked alive (or immediately after they are killed) because their flesh spoils quickly after they die. The simplest and most popular way to cook a live lobster is by boiling or steaming. After these basics, well, there's a whole lot to do with lobster beyond your standard roll. Herewith twenty-two recipes to satisfy your crustacean cravings.

Boiled Lobster

Choose a kettle large enough to hold all your lobsters and the water required to cook them (about 2 ½ quarts per lobster). Fill the pot one-half to two-thirds full with clean seawater or salted tap water (about 1 tablespoon of sea salt per quart). Bring water to a rolling boil. Place lobsters in the water head first one at a time. Cover the pot tightly, and begin timing when the water returns to a boil. Allow about eight minutes for 1-pound soft-shell lobsters and ten minutes for 1-pound hard-shell lobsters. Add one to two minutes for each additional quarter-pound. Lift the cooked lobsters out with tongs and let drain on a colander for a few minutes. Serve with drawn or melted butter for dipping.

Live lobsters —
one per person

Drawn or melted
butter (about ¼ cup
per 1-pound lobster)

Steamed Lobster

Live lobsters —
one per person

Drawn or melted
butter (about ¼ cup
per 1-pound lobster)

Choose a kettle large enough to hold all your lobsters. Fill the pot with about 2 inches of seawater or salted tap water (about 1 tablespoon sea salt per quart). Place a steamer rack in the pot, and bring the water to a rolling boil. Place lobsters in the pot and cover tightly. Start timing when the water returns to a boil. Allow about ten minutes for 1-pound soft-shell lobsters and twelve minutes for 1-pound hard-shell lobsters. Add one to two minutes for each additional quarter-pound. Lift the cooked lobsters out with tongs and let drain on a colander for a few minutes. Serve with drawn or melted butter for dipping.

Drawn Butter vs. Melted Butter

Some cooks prefer to serve their lobster with drawn butter rather than melted butter. What's the difference? Melted butter is just that: butter that has been melted. Drawn butter, also known as clarified butter, is melted butter from which the milk solids have been removed. This prevents the butter from burning and allows it to be heated to a higher temperature.

To make drawn butter: In a small saucepan, melt butter over medium heat. Bring to a boil until the milk solids separte and sink to the bottom of the pan. Ladle out the clarified butter.

① Unfold the plastic bib that came with your lobster. Notice how silly it is. Discard it. (Okay, wear it if you must, but be aware that it is akin to wearing a sign reading TOURIST.)

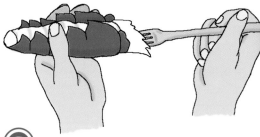

② Holding the lobster firmly by its back, twist off the claws at the first joint. Break the joints from the claws.

⑤ You will likely see some stuff that looks like soft green scrambled eggs in the body or carapace. This is tomalley, the lobster's digestive gland. Tomalley is considered a delicacy by some, however, the Gulf of Maine Research Institute Web site recommends discarding it because it has been found to contain high levels of mercury and other contaminants.

⑥ Cradling the tail belly side up in your hand, insert a fork into the shell and pull the meat out in one piece. If it's a tight fit, it may help to loosen the bend in the tail by flexing it until you hear it crack.

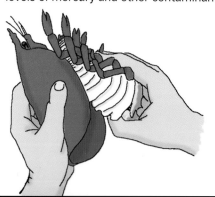

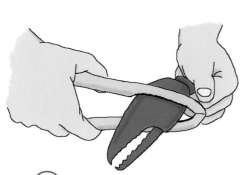

③ Crack the claw and joint pieces with a nutcracker and remove the meat, using a cocktail fork or pick as needed.

④ Grasp the back of the lobster in one hand and the tail in the other and twist in opposite directions to separate. Alternatively, you can bend the tail back from the body until it breaks free with a decisive crack, but this is likely to send lobster juices spraying across the table. Your dining companions will then curse you and the tip in Step 1.

⑦ Remove the legs and the smaller claws. Extract the meat by biting down on the pieces and squeezing the meat out with your teeth.

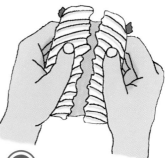

⑧ Unhinge the body from the shell. Open the underside of the body by cracking it apart in the middle. Poke around to find small chunks of meat inside the nooks and crannies.

Illustration by Emily Lilienthal

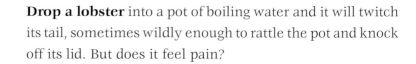

Drop a lobster into a pot of boiling water and it will twitch its tail, sometimes wildly enough to rattle the pot and knock off its lid. But does it feel pain?

Scientific study after scientific study have concluded that it does not, according to Bob Bayer, executive director of the Lobster Institute, a research and education organization at the University of Maine. Because lobsters have simple nervous systems similar to those of insects, they do not process pain, Bayer says. The tail movement, which typically continues for about a minute in boiling water, is a reflex reaction to the elevated water temperature.

That's not to say the lobsters don't feel anything. "They certainly have sensory structures, but the way their nervous system works is nothing like ours," says Diane Cowan of the Lobster Conservancy. "Lobsters regenerate parts — their nervous system is designed to shut off nerve impulses and shut off

The Pain

iStock Photo/
Robert Simon

blood vessels when they're injured at all the joints. If the lobster loses its claw, it stops bleeding and it stops sending nerve signals to that area. Its whole nervous system seems designed to shut down pain. That's how I like to think of it, but I really don't know. And I don't think it matters. I'm a locavore. I like to have venison from the island where I live, I like my own garden, I like wild plants. That lobster lived a good life in the wild. You have to appreciate your food and where it comes from and appreciate your place in nature."

So how to minimize a lobster's movements when placed in the cooking pot? Place it in the freezer or on ice for several minutes before dropping it in the pot, University of Maine researchers recommend. Lobsters that had been chilled before cooking moved for only about twenty seconds compared to a minute or more for lobsters boiled in the traditional manner. "Hypnotizing" a lobster by holding its head down and rubbing it and slow heating from room temperature both doubled the length of time it moves. ❖

HARD VS. SOFT

A 1-pound hard-shell lobster contains 4 to 5 ounces of meat. A 1-pound soft-shell lobster houses 2 to 3 ounces of meat — and a lot of water. Despite the smaller serving, soft-shell lobster has many fans, who swear the meat is sweeter. And soft-shell lobsters can be cracked apart without any tools.

Question

The Great Lobster Roll Debate

O n this most Mainers can agree: an authentic lobster roll is a top-loading hot-dog roll filled with chunks of cold cooked fresh lobster.

After that, the definition gets fuzzy. Should it be dressed with mayonnaise or butter or nothing at all? Can it be called a lobster roll if it contains celery and lettuce, a sprinkling of smoky paprika or, God forbid, finely diced cucumber, sliced scallions, and tarragon à la Chef Jasper White, a self-proclaimed New England food authority (wait; wasn't he born and raised in New Jersey?)? And who invented the scrumptious sandwich anyway?

Good questions all, and knowing how steamed aficionados get over what they consider lobster roll imposters, we're not about to offer definitive answers.

For one thing, there seem to be as many claims to the lobster roll's invention as there are ways to prepare it. One story holds that Harry Perry first served up lobster on a bun in his Milford, Connecticut, restaurant, now defunct, some time during the 1920s. The long-gone Nautilus Tea Room in Marblehead, Massachusetts, also has been credited with creating the sandwiches as a way of making use of culls (one-clawed lobsters). Bayley's Lobster Pound at Pine Point wisely stops short of declaring creatorship, boasting only that it was the first place in Maine to put lobster rolls on the menu. Without exact dates or documentation, we can't say who created this delightful version of lazy man's lobster, but we're glad they did.

Nutmeggers like their rolls filled with hot lobster drenched in melted butter, but cold or room temperature lobster is the norm elsewhere in New England. Here in Maine, the lobster roll is most commonly constructed by mixing the shellfish chunks — they should never be mashed to shreds with a fork like tuna — with the merest amount of mayonnaise. Offering a choice of mayo or drawn butter makes the kitchen's ring of authority.

Not just any hot-dog bun will do. It must be a New England style, or split-top, bun whose flat, crustless sides butter and grill beautifully, bringing out the bun's mild sweetness and warming it just enough to make a pleasing contrast to the cold lobster.

It's when cooks add extras — celery, lettuce, secret herb mixes — that enthusiasts' claws start snapping. This, they'll tell you, is a lobster salad sandwich; delicious it may be, but it is not a lobster roll. ✤

iStock Photo/Ha Huynh

The only essentials are lobster and a New England-style hot-dog bun. The rest is up for debate.

Rockland's
SEAFOOD CHALLENGE

A cooking contest has been part of the Maine Lobster Festival since it started in the 1940s. In the weeks before the festival begins, amateur cooks are challenged to submit recipes that use Maine seafood, and most contestants respond by creating something with lobster. Five finalists are selected and invited to cook their recipes at the festival for a panel of judges, who include a local chef, the Rockland mayor, and the commander of the visiting navy ship. In 2011, Russ James of Plainville, Connecticut, took first place with this recipe, which can be served as an elegant appetizer or as an entrée at a backyard picnic. More recipes from the festival contest appear on pages 129 and 131.

Pan Seared Sea Scallop & Lobster Medallions with Lemon Butter Sauce

4 lobsters, 1 ¼ pounds each

1 ½ pounds fresh large sea scallops

1 bunch of fresh broccolini (small heads of broccoli will do)

Sea salt, in a small cup for pinching

Fresh crushed black pepper in another cup

1 tablespoon extra virgin olive oil

½ pound butter

Lemon-butter sauce

This is a great way to introduce landlubbers to the classic rich flavor of New England seafood without the mess of nutcrackers and lobster bibs. Preparation time is about 40 minutes. *Serves 4.*

Put lobsters in large covered pot. Add 2 inches of water, just enough to steam them. When steam comes out, cook for 20 minutes and remove from heat. Spill lobsters out into sink and rinse with cold water. Set aside to cool.

While lobsters are cooking, spread out a five-sheet length of paper towels. Lay sea scallops atop the towels. Lay another five-sheet length atop the scallops and lightly press down to get them as dry as possible. Dust the tops and bottoms with salt and black pepper.

Pre-heat large saucepan until the edge is too hot to touch with the side of your hand. Add olive oil and one small cube of butter until melted. One by one place scallops into pan. Do not overcrowd them — you may need to cook them in batches. Flip them around with tongs as they become brown. Take care not to overcook them. (See tip on page 106.) When the scallops are done, remove from the pan, set aside in a covered bowl to keep them warm and moist, and sear the next batch. Add more oil and butter if the pan becomes dry.

HOW DO YOU KNOW...

...your scallops are ready? Let your fish guide you! Make a tight fist with your left hand. Use the index finger on your right hand to poke the soft meaty part of your left hand, just below the thumb. Tap the scallops with the tong. If they feel like that soft part of your hand, they're done. Remember, they will continue cooking for a short time.

Place a small steamer pot on to boil. Add the broccoli, cover and steam.

When the lobsters are cool enough to handle, remove the claws and pull out the breastplate. Pick the meat out of small legs and thoracic shell pockets. Use a spoon to scrape out the tomalley and red roe, if any, and set aside. Crack open claws, remove meat, and set aside.

Twist the tail section from the body. Use kitchen scissors to cut along the length of the underside of tail shell, front to back. Press down on shell edges to crack it open. Remove tail meat and set on cutting board. Remove the black vein by making a shallow slice down the bottom center of the tail. Press tail flat on cutting board and slice it into crosswise pieces, making thin round medallions, about one-quarter inch thick.

Use kitchen scissors to cut each of the four carapace shells. Trim along the edges to make a wider opening and trim the bottom so that it sits nicely upon the plate.

To plate, pile scallops and lobster medallions in center of plate. Crumble tomalley atop the pyramids. If you were lucky enough to have found red roe, use this as the crowning glory on each mound of succulent seafood.

Place the carapace, standing, as if to be offering its bounty. Stuff one broccolini stalk into the carapace so it delicately flowers over the seafood, looking like a spray of sea kelp. Drizzle lemon-butter sauce over the entire seafood medley, until it makes a golden pool of deliciousness in the plate.

Lemon-Butter Sauce

1 cup Riesling wine

¼ cup finely chopped shallots

¼ teaspoon white pepper

1 teaspoon white sugar

¼ cup cream sherry

½ fresh lemon, squeezed and juiced

2 tablespoons heavy cream

8 ounces (two sticks) cold butter, cut into ¼ inch cubes

This sauce is easy to make and has a rich, mellow flavor that is delicious with any seafood. Use it while it is warm on cod, scallops, lobster, or other white fish. Throw away leftovers because after it cools, the sauce separates and does not taste the same when reheated. Cooking time is about 15 minutes. *Serves 4.*

Pre-heat a large saucepan. Add wine, lemon juice, and shallots. Bring mixture to a mildly bubbling simmer over medium heat. Stir occasionally until mixture is reduced by about one-quarter. Turn heat to lowest setting.

Whisk in the heavy cream. Add four or five small cubes of butter and gently "rub" them into the mixture with the whisk. After the cubes have melted into the hot reduction, add another four or five cubes and repeat the process until all the butter is melted. The cold butter is used to flavor and cool the mix.

Turn off the heat. Add white pepper, sugar, and cream sherry and gently whisk until the mixture takes on a pure ivory color.

Craig Dilger

Three chefs vie to win the hearts of two hundred diners every fall at the Lobster Chef of the Year competition during Harvest on the Harbor, the Greater Portland Convention and Visitors Bureau's popular food and wine event in Portland, Maine. Sponsored by the Maine Lobster Council, the cook-off challenges chefs to create new and delectable ways to serve Maine's signature shellfish.

Lobster Chef of the Year

In the weeks before the competition, two of Maine's top chefs sift through recipes submitted by their peers and choose the three finalists. During the contest, which is held in the kitchenless Ocean Gateway ship terminal, the contestants must cook their dishes in twenty minutes before an audience of two hundred people, who serve as the final judges.

In 2011, the audience chose Slow-Poached Maine Lobster Tail Nipponese, made by Tom Reagan, a private chef from Kennebunkport who originally created the dish as an appetizer for a client. This dish consists of a lobster tail poached in lemon-butter sauce served atop a rice cake coated in black and white sesame seeds with an orange miso coleslaw garnish.

"I had worked in the past with Japanese flavors, so I knew that orange, miso, ginger, mirin, tamari, and sesame seeds were a good mix," Reagan says. "I also wanted to be true to Maine lobster, so I went with a traditional lemon-butter sauce."

Craig Dilger

Slow Poached Maine Lobster Tail Nipponese

Slow poaching Maine lobster tails in a butter sauce is a unique approach to lobster cookery that results in a very tender, melt-in-your-mouth texture. This recipe can be adapted for a starter course, fish course in a multi-course dinner, or an entrée. The portion presented here calls for a four-ounce lobster tail as a starter course. Please read recipes through completely before commencing. Some preparation a day or two prior to service is more efficient, especially if the chef wants to enjoy this meal with guests.

LOBSTER TAIL PREPARATION

Four 1 ½-pound,
hard-shell lobsters

Steam whole lobster for two minutes then remove from pot with tongs. Twist tail off body. Remove par-cooked tail meat, whole. Clean tail of tomalley remnants. Remove intestinal vein (optional). Skewer tail to maintain shape before poaching. Save claws and knuckles to make stew or lobster rolls.

LEMON-BUTTER SAUCE

½ cup seasoned rice
wine vinegar

¼ cup dry white wine

3 teaspoons minced
shallot

¼ cup heavy cream

1 cup unsalted butter,
cubed, cold

2 tablespoons freshly
squeezed lemon juice

pinch salt

Reduce vinegar and wine with shallots to a syrup consistency in saucepan on medium heat about five minutes. Add heavy cream to reduction. Reduce cream for a minute until thickened. Whisk in cold butter one cube at a time until fully incorporated and just starting to simmer. Whisk in lemon juice and salt to taste. This is the slow poaching liquid. Keep liquid very warm, approximately 150 F. Place lobster tails in sauce and return to simmer. Cover and remove from heat, let stand about 10 minutes. Return to heat for a minute or two prior to service.

RICE CAKE

4 cups cooked sushi
rice, according to
package instructions,
still hot

¼ cup mirin

¼ cup rice wine
vinegar

2 tablespoons honey

1 tablespoon black
sesame seeds

1 tablespoon white
sesame seeds

Place hot rice in a stainless bowl. Add all ingredients except seeds. Blend very well with rubber spatula. Place mixture in small glass baking dish, pack firmly, cover with plastic wrap, and refrigerate until thoroughly chilled. Mixture should be about one inch deep and may not fill entire dish. Best if left overnight to chill.

Mix black and white sesame seeds together, spread over pie pan or other flat surface. Cut cooled rice mixture into two-inch strips and remove dish. Cut into desired shape with sharp chef knife. Garnish sides of rice cakes by pressing onto seeds. Rice cakes can be made several days in advance. Refrigerate to store.

To serve, place on sheet pan, heat at 400 F for 10 minutes.

ORANGE MISO COLESLAW

Dressing:

Zest of 1 orange

1 cup freshly
squeezed orange
(approximately four
juicy oranges)

To make the dressing: Zest one orange then juice all oranges, strain out pulp, and place in saucepan with ginger and garlic. Reduce to 1/4 cup of orange syrup. Put syrup and remaining ingredients, except vegetable oil and salt, in blender. On high speed slowly add oil to emulsify. Season dressing with just a pinch of salt if needed. Funnel into squeeze bottle for service. Coleslaw dressing can be made several days in advance.

1 teaspoon grated ginger

½ teaspoon grated garlic

½ teaspoon wasabi paste

¾ teaspoons tamari

2 teaspoons white miso

1 teaspoon honey

1 tablespoon plus 1 teaspoon rice wine vinegar

1 tablespoon mirin

½ cup vegetable oil

pinch of salt

Refrigerate to store. Bring to room temperature before service. Shake well before using.

To make the slaw: Wash carrot, zucchini, and squash. Peel carrot and fine julienne it using mandoline into 1 1/2-inch lengths. Use mandoline to julienne the outer portion of the zucchini and squash, the same size as the carrot, being conscious to maintain a uniform and colorful peel. Shred or finely slice cabbages. Finely slice mushroom caps. Toss vegetables and mushrooms in a stainless bowl to mix ingredients. Refrigerate covered until needed. Mix can be made a day in advance.

Fifteen minutes before service, toss vegetable mix with miso dressing to taste, about one-third cup. Check seasoning.

Coleslaw:

1 small zucchini

1 carrot

1 summer squash

1 cup shredded Savoy cabbage

1 cup shredded red cabbage

2 or 3 shitake mushrooms, caps only

Plating: Place rice cake in center of plate. Artfully place tail on rice cake. Garnish with coleslaw. Drizzle small amount of lemon-butter sauce and coleslaw dressing on plate and lobster. Serve immediately.

Craig Dilger

Maine Lobster

Bake

The traditional lobster bake takes place on the beach and is a daylong affair. *Serves 10.*

FOOD

Ten 1 ¼-pound live lobsters

5 dozen littleneck or cherrystone clams, scrubbed

5 dozen mussels, scrubbed and de-bearded

10 ears of corn, outer husks and silk removed

30 small red potatoes, scrubbed

30 small onions, peeled

melted butter

FOR THE PIT:

Seaweed, preferably rockweed — about five, 30-gallon garbage bags full

Large smooth stones to line the pit

Driftwood or cordwood, including kindling and logs no more than 5 inches in diameter

Large canvas tarp or a couple yards of burlap, thoroughly soaked with seawater.

Dig a pit in the sand about 1 ½ feet deep, 2 feet wide, and 3 feet long. Line the bottom of the pit with the stones, then build a big fire with the wood on top of the stones. Feed the fire to keep it going for 1 to 2 hours, then allow it to burn down to coals, about an hour.

While the fire burns, soak the corncobs in water. When the coals are ready, cover the stones with a 6- to 8-inch layer of seaweed. Place the lobsters on top of the seaweed. Layer the ingredients in the following order: potatoes, onions, corn, clams, and mussels. Top with a 3- to 4-inch layer of seaweed. (Note: Some cooks like to wrap the ingredients in cheesecloth to make large bundles, which are easier to remove from the fire.) Cover with the wet tarp or burlap, using rocks to hold it in place. Cook 45 minutes to one hour. Lift the tarp at one corner and see if the lobsters are bright red and the mussels and clams have opened. If so, your feast is ready. Remove the food and serve hot with melted butter.

Red's Eats World Famous Lobster Roll

Fresh meat from one 1 ¼ to 1 ½ pound hard-shell lobster or two to three 1 ¼-pound soft shell lobsters, including two whole claws and a whole tail, deveined, and split

1 split hot-dog bun, sides brushed with melted butter

Drawn butter (optional)

Mayonnaise, preferably Hellmann's extra heavy (optional)

No lobster roll has received more publicity than the one served by Red's Eats, the tiny red lobster shack with the long lines in the heart of Wiscasset village. After hearing the words "hold the mayo" over and over, the late Al Gagnon, a.k.a."Red," began stuffing his grilled buns with an ultra-generous serving of unadorned lobster, and offering mayonnaise and drawn butter on the side. Recipe from *Red's Eats: World's Best Lobster Shack* by Virginia M. Wright and Debbie Gagnon Cronk (Down East Books, 2010).

Grill the hot-dog bun until sides are toasted and golden. Rip lobster meat into chunks by hand (do not use a knife; it imparts an oxidized flavor to seafood) and fill the middle of the roll. Put the whole claws at each end of the roll so they are dangling over the edge. Place a split lobster tail on top. Eat as is or drizzled with drawn butter or mayonnaise.

Nance Trueworthy

Marjorie Standish's Baked Stuffed Lobster

The late Marjorie Standish was a cookbook author and the longtime editor of the "Cooking Down East" column for the *Maine Sunday Telegram,* the state's largest-circulation Sunday paper. This recipe is from the revised edition of *Cooking Down East: Favorite Maine Recipes* (Down East Books, 2010).

TO SPLIT A LIVE LOBSTER:
Place the lobster on its back. Cross the large claws over its head and hold firmly with your left hand. Make a deep, quick incision with a sharp pointed knife and draw the knife quickly down the entire length of the body and tail.

TO CLEAN LOBSTER:
Spread the lobster flat. Using a teaspoon, remove the tomalley. This will go into the stuffing. So will the coral or roe, if it happens to be a female lobster. The next step is to break the intestinal vein where it is attached to the end of the tail. Use the handle of the spoon to do this.

Before you remove this vein there is another step: Use your fingers to remove the sac or stomach (a lobster's stomach is under its head). Using two fingers, remove this sac in one fell swoop. As you do this, it will break the other end of the intestinal

SEEING RED

Lobsters turn red when they are cooked because the process masks all of their many different color pigments called chromatophores, except the red background pigment called astaxanthin.

tract. Now, use the teaspoon handle again and complete the removal of this tract.

Make sure the cavity is cleaned out; you may do this by holding under running cold water. Turn lobster over and allow to drain. It is now ready for stuffing.

STUFFING:

For eight lobsters use the following amount:

½ pound butter, melted

2 cups dried bread-crumbs, ground fine (make this a generous amount)

2 teaspoons Worcestershire Sauce

a little salt

tomalley and coral, too

Preheat oven to 325°F. Mix all together. Fill cavity of lobster with the stuffing, using a spoon for this. Divide the amount of stuffing among the number of lobsters you are baking, using amounts above as a guide. With this amount of butter in stuffing, no need to "dot" any on top. For a drier stuffing, use more breadcrumbs.

Place stuffed lobsters in foil-lined pan. Alternate heads and tails so they will fit better in pan. Bring edge of foil up over end of tail of each lobster. Press foil, so it secures end of tail firmly to edge of pan. If you do not do this, tails are apt to curl up as they bake. Remove rubber bands from claws.

Bake for 50 minutes, depending upon size of lobsters.

Marjorie Standish's Lobster Newburg

2 cups lobster meat,
cut in medium-size
pieces

4 tablespoons butter

1 tablespoon flour

1 cup light cream

2 egg yolks, beaten

1 tablespoon lemon
juice

¼ teaspoon salt

paprika

Another traditional Maine recipe from Marjorie Standish's *Cooking Down East: Favorite Maine Recipes* (Down East Books, 2010). *Serves 4.*

Melt 3 tablespoons butter, add lobster meat, and cook slowly to start the pink color; use a low heat for doing this. In another saucepan, melt the remaining tablespoon of butter, add flour, salt, a dash of paprika. Add cream or evaporated milk, stirring constantly; cook over low heat until thickened. Remove from heat, turn in beaten egg yolks. Turn back into pan, return to heat, and stir again until thickened. Add the heated lobster and lemon juice. Serve at once on toast points.

Lobster Pie

2 tablespoons butter

¼ cup sherry

1 cup well-packed raw lobster meat

¾ cup light cream

3 tablespoons butter

1 tablespoon flour

2 egg yokes

This recipe is from *Maine Coastal Cooking and The Accomplished Cook or The Whole Art and Mystery of Cookery, Fitted for all Degrees and Qualities.* (Down East Books, 1980), a collection of recipes dating from 1664.

Add sherry to 2 tablespoons melted butter; boil one minute. Add lobster and let stand. Melt 3 tablespoons butter; add flour and stir until it bubbles 1 minute. Remove from heat; slowly stir in cream and wine drained from lobster. Return to heat and cook, stirring constantly until sauce is smooth and thick. Remove from heat.

Heat the sauce in top of a double boiler over hot but not boiling water. (The sauce may curdle if the water boils.) Stir constantly while heating, about 3 minutes. Remove from heat; add lobster. Turn into small deep pie plate. Sprinkle with topping and bake in 300 degree oven for 10 minutes.

Topping: Mix ¼ cup cracker meal, 1/4 teaspoon paprika, 1 tablespoon finely crushed potato chips, and 1 1/2 tablespoons Parmesan cheese. Add 2 tablespoons melted butter and blend well.

Marjorie Mosser's Lobster Stew

1 boiled lobster, about 1 to 1 ½ pounds

crackers

chicken stock to moisten

1 quart whole milk

butter, to taste

salt and pepper, to taste

This recipe comes from one of the bibles of traditional Maine cookery, *Good Maine Food: Ancient and Modern New England Food & Drink* by Marjorie Mosser, first published in the 1930s and revised by Down East Books in 2010.

Pick meat from a boiled lobster and chop it fine with crackers. Add chicken stock to moisten. For each pint of lobster mixture, add a quart of rich milk. Season with butter, salt, and pepper.

Marjorie Mosser's Lobster Bisque

2 medium lobsters, undercooked

2 cups water

1 quart milk

6 tablespoons butter

2 tablespoons flour

2 cups oyster crackers rolled to a dust

1 teaspoon salt

few grains cayenne

Another classic from *Good Maine Food: Ancient and Modern New England Food & Drink* by Marjorie Mosser (Down East Books, 2010). Serves 6.

Remove meat from shell and large claws and pass through fine grinder. Break body and small claws, cover with water, bring slowly to boiling point, and cook 20 minutes. Drain and add liquor to milk and scald. Melt butter; stir in flour and cracker crumbs; gradually stir in hot liquid and cook 5 minutes, stirring till smooth and thickened. Add seasonings and lobster meat, and heat thoroughly. Add remaining butter and serve.

Lobster Chowder

2 cups lobster meat

4 tablespoons butter

1 cup water

2 cups hot milk

2 cups diced raw potatoes

1 small onion, sliced

paprika

salt and pepper

This recipe is from *Maine Coastal Cooking and The Accomplished Cook or The Whole Art and Mystery of Cookery, Fitted for all Degrees and Qualities.* (Down East Books, 1980), a collection of recipes dating from 1664.

Simmer the lobster meat in the butter over low heat for 7 or 8 minutes. Combine potatoes, onion, and water and boil until tender. Add hot milk and lobster mixture. Season to taste and add a dash of paprika.

iStock Photo/Greg Nicholas

Herb Grilled Maine Lobster Tail on Arugula with Chive Ricotta Gnocchi & Corn Milk

4 raw lobster tails in shell

4 ounces unsalted butter

½ teaspoon minced thyme

½ teaspoon minced chive

½ teaspoon minced rosemary

salt and pepper to taste

sea salt, pinch per tail

Kelly Patrick Farrin, the sous chef at Azure Café in Freeport, Maine, won the Maine Lobster Council's 2010 Lobster Chef of the Year competition with this recipe. *Serves 4.*

GRILLED MAINE LOBSTER TAIL
(preparation time: 5 minutes)

Cut with sharp knife down the middle underside of each tail lengthwise, remove intestinal debris. Leave lobster meat in halved shell. Remove all small "feeler legs" from underside of each tail.

In small saucepan add butter, thyme, chives, rosemary, and salt and pepper to taste. Bring to simmer and reserve. Rub lobster tail with sea salt and grill, meat side down first, for 2½ minutes. Flip lobster tails and brush meat with herb-infused butter. Cook for 2 to 2½ more minutes. Reserve excess herb-infused butter.

Focus Photography

WILTED ARUGULA
(preparation time: 5 minutes)

4 cups packed, fresh arugula

1 tablespoon extra virgin olive oil

½ cup quartered grape tomatoes

1 teaspoon minced garlic

2 teaspoons fresh lemon juice

salt and pepper to taste

Wash arugula in cold water, place in salad spinner to remove excess water. Cut grape tomatoes into quarters, length and width cut. Bring sauté pan to medium heat. Add olive oil and garlic to sauté pan. Cook just until it begins to change color.

Immediately add grape tomatoes. Cook 1 minute. Add arugula to sauté pan, toss with tongs for 1 minute. Finish with fresh lemon juice and salt and pepper to taste. Remove from pan, leaving behind excess liquid.

Heat sauté pan over medium-high heat. Add butter and gently place gnocchi in pan. Brown each side for a crispy outer shell. Finish with salt and pepper to taste.

CHIVE RICOTTA GNOCCHI
(preparation time: 15 minutes)

1 cup ricotta cheese

2 egg yolks

½ cup shredded Parmesan cheese

pinch nutmeg

2 teaspoons lemon zest

Mix ricotta cheese, egg yolks, Parmesan cheese, nutmeg, lemon zest, chives, and salt together in mixing bowl with rubber spatula. Fully combine. Slowly add sifted all-purpose flour to ricotta mix. Fold small amounts of flour into wet ingredients until it forms and becomes a soft dough. Reserve excess flour. Once soft dough is formed, let sit in covered bowl for 5 minutes to rest.

Place dough on clean, floured countertop to reduce sticking. Knead dough until smooth and elastic. Cut dough into 4 equal parts and roll with fingers to form long and round, ½-inch thick

2 tablespoons
minced chives

¾ cup all-purpose
flour

½ tablespoon salt

2 ounces butter

ropes. Cut dough into ¾-inch segments and reserve on floured baking sheet, make sure gnocchi are not touching each other.

Bring a large pot of salted water to a boil. Place gnocchi in water, and with a wooden spoon, carefully stir to separate. Then boil for 5 minutes. Remove gnocchi from heat and pour into colander. Lightly coat with olive oil. Pour onto sheet pan and cool in refrigerator.

CORN MILK PURÉE
(preparation time: 10 minutes)

2 ears corn on cob

salt to taste

Shuck and clean corn. Remove kernels from cob with knife, cutting downwards into the pith of the cob. Place kernels in food processor and pulse until macerated. Pass corn purée through fine mesh strainer (chinois). Use the bottom of a ladle and press until purée is almost dry. Reserve liquid, discard pulp. Heat double boiler and place corn liquid in bowl. Heat until it thickens. Place in small squirt bottle or use teaspoon to sauce plates.

TO SERVE:
Place butter-seared gnocchis in center of plate. Next, use tongs to place wilted arugula on top of gnocchi. Arrange 2 grilled half lobster tails together and place on top of arugula. Spoon extra herb-infused butter over grilled lobster tails and shell. Finish with circular pours of corn milk around plate. Garnish with fresh rosemary.

Roasted Maine Lobster Tail on Braised Cabbage and Cornbread

½ ounce unsalted butter

4 ounces bacon, small diced

1 cup onions, small diced

½ tablespoon garlic, minced

½ tablespoon shallots, minced

2 pounds cabbage, stems removed, roughly torn

2¼ ounces white wine

5½ ounces chicken stock

1 ham hock

salt and pepper, to taste

MacKenzie Arrington took first place in the Maine Lobster Council's 2009 Lobster Chef of the Year competition with this recipe. *Serves 4.*

BRAISED CABBAGE

Render bacon in butter until light golden brown in a wide sauce pot. Add onions and garlic, sweat until aromatic. Add cabbage and sweat until aromatic. Deglaze with wine, reduce by half. Add chicken stock and ham hock, cover, bring to simmer and braise until tender, about 40 minutes. Remove cabbage and reserve. Reduce braising liquid to glace. Remove ham hock. Add cabbage back to braising liquid. Season to taste with salt and pepper. Reserve for production.

Focus Photography

ROASTED LOBSTER TAILS

4 lobster tails, split

2 tablespoons
unsalted butter

shallots, minced

2 cloves garlic,
minced

salt and pepper

Split each tail with scissors along the top of the shell. Remove intestinal tract. In a sauté pan melt butter and sweat shallots and garlic. Lightly brush lobster tail meat with melted butter mixture. Place the tails on a medium-high temp grill meat side up. Flip after 5 minutes. Flip again after 3 minutes and lightly reapply butter mixture. Cook for another couple minutes until done. Reserve for production.

CORNBREAD

⅔ cup unsalted
butter, softened

1 cup sugar (half if
too sweet)

3 eggs

3 ounces sweet corn

1 cup cornmeal

2⅓ cups all-purpose flour

4½ teaspoons baking
soda (more if not fluffy)

1 teaspoon salt

Preheat oven to 400 F. Cream soft butter and sugar. Combine milk and eggs. Combine all dry ingredients. Add dry ingredients to creamed mixture alternately with egg mixture. Pour into a greased cast iron skillet. Bake for 20 – 27 minutes or until toothpick test is successful. Cut into rounds for production.

COMPOUND BUTTER

8 tablespoons
unsalted butter

½ tablespoons pars-
ley, minced

½ tablespoon tarra-
gon, minced

¼ tablespoon thyme,
minced

¼ tablespoon chervil,
minced

¼ tablespoon chives,
minced

1 teaspoon lemon
juice

salt, to taste

Cream butter and herbs together until herbs are fully incorporated. Add lemon juice and salt to taste. Transfer butter and herb
mixture to plastic wrap and shape into a 1-inch- diameter log.
Roll butter tightly and place into freezer until production.

TO SERVE:
Place cornbread round as a base in the center of the plate. Top
with a layer of braised cabbage and bacon. Place the roasted lobster tail on the cabbage. Top with a ¼ slice of compound butter.

Thai-accented Lobster and Native Corn Bisque

Richard Lemoine, executive chef at the Cape Arundel Inn in Kennebunkport, created this combination of lobster, vegetables, coconut milk, and Thai seasonings. From *The Eat Local Cookbook: Seasonal Recipes from a Maine Farm* by Lisa Turner (Down East Books, 2011). *Serves 4.*

Cook in a pot of boiling, lightly salted water:
2 ears corn

Drain, cool, and cut the kernels off the cob and set aside.

In a large stockpot over medium heat, melt:
2 tablespoons butter

Add and sauté until fragrant, about 8 minutes:
1 small carrot, peeled and diced

½ red pepper, diced

2 stalks celery, diced

2 garlic cloves, crushed

2 teaspoons peeled and minced fresh ginger

Add and stir to make a paste:
½ cup flour

Slowly add to the paste, stirring constantly:

2 cups chicken stock

2 cups seafood or vegetable stock

½ cup sherry

Bring to a simmer and cook for about 20 minutes, skimming any foam off the top. Add:

6 basil leaves, chopped

3 tablespoons chopped cilantro leaves

one (13.5-ounce) can coconut milk

4 tablespoons sweet chili Thai sauce

a few drops toasted sesame oil

salt

freshly ground black pepper

Simmer for 3 minutes more and turn off the heat. Cool for half an hour, then blend with a blender, food processor, or immersion blender. Put the soup back on the stove and add the corn kernels and:

2 cups lobster meat, cooked and chopped

Heat just through and serve.

Lobster and Crab Galette

8 ounces fresh lobster meat, chopped into ¼- to ½-inch pieces

8 ounces Maine crab meat

1 prepared piecrust

1 egg

1 egg yolk

3 tablespoons mayonnaise

½ teaspoon seafood seasoning

2–3 dashes of hot sauce

¼ cup celery diced

¼ cup shallot diced

¼ cup unsalted crackers, smashed

¼ cup Gruyère cheese, grated

The second-place winner in the Maine Lobster Festival Seafood Cooking Contest, this recipe was created by Sue Jobes of Davie, Florida. Preparation and cooking time is about 1 1/2 hours. *Serves 4.*

Preheat oven to 375°F.

Heat olive oil in a skillet. Add the celery and anchovy filets and sauté for about two minutes. Add the shallots and lightly sprinkle with salt and pepper. Sauté until the shallots are translucent. Add the chopped garlic. When you smell the garlic fragrance, pour in the sherry. Let the sherry reduce until almost dry. Remove the pan from the heat and stir in the herbs. Set aside and let the ingredients cool.

Combine the whole egg and mayonnaise. Whisk until smooth. Add the seafood seasoning, cheese, and cracker crumbs. Stir until combined.

Add the lobster and crab to the egg-crumbs mixture. Toss gently to combine. Add the vegetables-herb mixture and combine. Set aside.

Roll out the dough to half its original thickness. Using a bowl (or round pastry cutter), make four circles of dough 5 to 6 inches in diameter.

1 large anchovy

2 tablespoons parsley, finely chopped

1 tablespoon basil, finely chopped

1 large garlic clove, minced

1–2 tablespoons olive oil

1–2 tablespoons sherry (or chicken stock)

1 lemon for garnish

salt and pepper

TOPPING:

2 tablespoons mayonnaise

1–2 tablespoons cream

¼ teaspoon seafood seasoning

¼ teaspoon paprika

Place one-quarter of the seafood mixture in the center of each dough circle. Fold the pie dough up and pleat around the seafood mixture.

Whisk the egg yolk with 1 teaspoon of water. Using a pastry brush, brush dough with yolk.

Combine the topping ingredients and place a small dollop on top of seafood.

Bake for 20 minutes at 375°F. Remove from oven and let cool for 10 to 15 minutes before serving.

Breezy Lobster Curry Mac 'n' Cheese with Crispy Crab Topping

Two 16-ounce packages of rotini, cooked al dente and drained

8 ounces sharp white cheddar cheese, grated

8 ounces Jarlsberg cheese, grated

8 ounces Jack cheese, grated

Two 1 1/4-pound lobsters, steamed, picked, and cooled

2 tablespoons butter

1 tablespoon dry sherry

1 teaspoon curry powder

Created by Carol W. Bachofner of Rockland, Maine, this recipe took third place in the 2011 Maine Lobster Festival Seafood Cooking Contest. *Serves 6.*

Preheat oven to 375°F.

Butter a 2-quart glass or ceramic baking dish.

In large glass mixing bowl, combine pasta and lobster meat.

Cover the bottom of the baking dish with a layer of pasta. Spread the Jarlsberg cheese over the pasta. Add another layer of pasta, and spread the cheddar cheese over it. Add another layer of pasta, finishing with the Jack cheese.

In glass mixing bowl, combine evaporated milk with sherry, curry, butter, and dry mustard. Pour this mixture evenly over the top of the pasta-cheese layers. Cover with foil and bake.

While it cooks, make the crispy crab topping. After the casserole has baked for thirty minutes, remove it from the oven and sprinkle the topping over it. Raise the oven temperature to 400°F and bake the casserole, uncovered, for an additional ten minutes or until the topping crisps.

1 teaspoon dry
mustard

12 ounces evapo-
rated milk

TOPPING:

8 ounces fresh crab-
meat, crumbled

1 cup coarse bread
crumbs

½ cup Parmesan
cheese, grated

2 tablespoons butter,
melted

CRISPY CRAB TOPPING

Combine all the dry ingredients and toss with melted butter.

Japanese Lobster Rolls

1 daikon (Japanese white radish)

1 carrot

1 cup clover or alfalfa sprouts

3 scallions

2 tablespoons mayonnaise

1 teaspoon wasabi powder

½ teaspoon sesame oil

pinch salt

meat from 1 1/4 pound lobster

4 tablespoons sliced pickled ginger

This twist on the traditional lobster roll is from *Far East Down East* by Bruce DeMustchine (Down East Books, 2003). *Serves 4.*

Peel the daikon and cut in half lengthwise. With a vegetable peeler or a mandoline, cut from the center (cut side) of each half at least 12 very thin slices measuring 6 inches long and 2 inches wide. The slices need to be thin — 1/16 inch or less — so they will not crack when rolled.

Peel the carrot and cut it lengthwise into 4 slices about 1/8 inch thick. Then cut each slice into strips and cut the strips into 4-inch-long pieces. Rinse and drain the sprouts. Trim the root end from the scallions. Otherwise, leave them whole.

Pour water into a medium skillet until it is a quarter full. Bring to a gentle boil over low heat and add the scallions. Let the water come back to a boil, then turn off the heat. Allow the scallions to stand in the hot water for 10 minutes.

In the meantime, whisk together the mayonnaise, wasabi powder, sesame oil, and salt. Cut the lobster meat into pieces about 1 ½ inches long.

Remove the cooked scallions from the water and gently slip the leaves apart, removing the outer ones first.

To assemble, place a slice of daikon horizontally on a flat surface. Put 1/2 teaspoon of the wasabi mixture in the center. Place

2 carrot sticks on top so they protrude over the top edge of the daikon. Place a small bunch of the sprouts on top of the carrot sticks, then arrange some of the lobster meat on top of the sprouts.

Starting from the left side of the slice of daikon, roll into a tight bundle, taking care that the daikon does not crack. Take one of the softened scallion leaves and tie it around the middle of each roll to hold it together.

Chill for 20 minutes. Garnish each serving with 1 tablespoon pickled ginger.

Grilled Thai Chili Lobster

4 cloves garlic

3 shallots

2 small fresh red chilies

2 small fresh green chilies

½ cup chopped cilantro

two 2-pound uncooked lobsters

From *Far East Down East* by Bruce DeMustchine (Down East Books, 2003). *Serves 4.*

Finely slice the garlic and shallots. Seed and finely slice the red and green chilies. Coarsely chop the cilantro.

Pour 3 to 4 inches of water into a very large pot; bring to a boil. Add the live lobsters and let the water return to a boil. Cook for 2 minutes, then remove from the heat and carefully pour away all but 1 inch of water. Return to the heat, place a lid to almost cover the pot, and steam the lobsters for 12 minutes. Remove the lobsters and allow them to cool long enough to handle.

Start a grill or broiler and get it up to a high heat. Cut the cooked lobsters in half, down the center of the back. Remove

2 tablespoons veg-
etable oil

2 tablespoons fish
sauce

½ teaspoon freshly
ground black pepper

the claws; crack them open, remove all the meat, and cut it into bite-size pieces. Clean out the body cavity and discard the inedible bits. Remove the tail meat from the shell and carefully slice it, taking care to keep the tail shell together. Return the tail meat to the shell. Place the cut-up claw meat into the body cavity.

Heat the oil in a small pan. Add the sliced garlic and cook gently, taking care not to burn it. As the garlic starts to brown, add the sliced shallots and chilies, the fish sauce, and the ground pepper. Stir and cook gently for a few seconds.

Spoon the chili mixture evenly over the four lobster halves. Place the lobsters on the preheated grill or under the broiler and cook for 3 to 4 minutes.

Transfer to four dinner plates and sprinkle with the chopped cilantro.

Kathy Gunst's Angry Lobster

four (1-pound) live
lobsters

coarse sea salt

freshly ground black
pepper

¼ cup olive oil

Kathy Gunst credits her friend, chef Neil Kleinberg, for this recipe, part of her *Notes from a Maine Kitchen* (Down East Books, 2011) collection. Gunst writes, "This is not for the weak of heart: a live lobster is chopped into bite-size pieces, tossed with olive oil, garlic, basil, rosemary, and crushed red pepper and roasted in a hot oven." Serve with pasta and garlic bread. *Serves 4.*

8 large cloves garlic, very thinly sliced

1 cup fresh basil leaves, torn into large pieces

2 to 3 sprigs fresh rosemary, cut into 2-inch pieces (stem and herb)

1 teaspoon crushed red pepper flakes

Place the live lobster on a work surface shell side down. Using a large sharp knife, make an incision where the tail and body connect, with the blade facing the head of the lobster. Push down the knife, cutting the body into two pieces. (This will kill the lobsters instantly.) Using your hands, twist the tail off and pull off the claws, removing the rubber bands. Separate the body into halves, then cut into quarters, slicing across the body. Remove and discard the stomach sac at the top of the head. Remove the tomalley and set aside.

Cut the tail into four pieces. Separate the knuckles from the claws. With a quick action, use the back of the knife to crack the top of the claw. Turn the knife over and cut the claw in half at the joint. Make a small incision in the soft bottom part of the knuckle and cut in half. At the end of the process you should have 16 pieces of lobster. Repeat with the remaining lobsters.

Place the lobster pieces in a large bowl and season with salt and pepper.

Preheat the oven to 450°F. Place a large shallow roasting pan in the hot oven and preheat for 5 to 10 minutes, or until very hot.

Remove the preheated pan from the oven and carefully add the oil to the pan. (Careful, it may splatter.) Place the lobster pieces in the hot pan, shell side down, and roast for 6 minutes, or until the shells turn red. Sprinkle the garlic on the bottom of the pan (you want it to brown) and then sprinkle the top of the lobsters with the basil, rosemary, and crushed red pepper. Roast another 6 to 8 minutes, or until the lobster is cooked through but still tender.

Dana Moos' Egg Roulade Filled with Sautéed Leeks and Parmesan, Topped with Lobster, Sherry, and Melted Butter

8 eggs

2 cups plus 2 table-spoons heavy cream

1 teaspoon salt

2 tablespoons extra virgin olive oil

3 large leeks, washed and thinly sliced

one (8-ounce) pack-age cream cheese

1 teaspoon Worces-tershire sauce

juice from one-quar-ter lemon

1 stick plus 3 table-spoons butter

1½ cups shredded Parmesan cheese

The signature savory dish at the Pomegranate Inn in Port-land, Maine, this recipe is from innkeeper Dana Moos' *The Art of Breakfast* (Down East Books, 2011). "This is one of the most indulgent entrées we served," she writes, "but it was worth every calorie and penny." Serves 4 to 6.

Preheat the oven to 350°F.

Grease a rimmed heavy-duty half sheet pan with butter or vegetable oil, then line with parchment paper, and then grease the parchment, making sure to press it flat to the surface of the pan, leaving at least an inch of overhang.

In a blender, mix the eggs, 2 cups of cream, and ½ teaspoon salt on high speed for four to five seconds. Pour the mixture into the lined baking sheet. Bake until you begin to see the surface of the egg just start to brown, about twenty minutes. Remove and let cool.

While cooling, heat the olive oil in a pan over medium-high heat. Sauté the leeks, covered, until soft, about 10 to 12 minutes. When soft, add the cream cheese, Worcestershire sauce, the remaining 2 tablespoons of cream, lemon juice, and the remain-ing 1/2 teaspoon of salt and stir. When the cream cheese is thor-oughly incorporated, add three tablespoons of butter, mix in, and remove from heat. Let cool for about 3 minutes.

½ cup dry sherry

16 ounces fresh, cooked lobster meat, cut into small chunks

one (10-ounce) package baby spinach, washed and dried

fresh chopped chives, for garnish

Dollop small amounts of the leek filling onto the egg. Using an offset spatula, carefully spread the mixture over the entire egg sponge, trying not to tear the egg as it is very delicate. Sprinkle the Parmesan over the filling.

Here's the fun part: the rolling. With the short edge of the pan closest to you, using the parchment as a guide, roll the egg up onto itself (like a Hostess Ho-Hos!) until you end up with the egg seam on the underside of the roll. Keep the egg covered with the parchment left after rolling as it will help keep the egg moist. Cover the entire roll with aluminum foil and bake for another 20 minutes.

While baking, melt the remaining stick of butter in a pan with the sherry and cook for about 5 minutes, allowing much of the alcohol to evaporate. Then add the lobster, lower the heat, and cover. Simmer for 5 minutes.

To serve, place a pile of fresh baby spinach on a plate. Slice the roulade into 4 to 6 slices, layer onto the spinach, and top with a couple of spoonfuls of the lobster butter. Garnish with fresh chives.

Melissa Kelley's Lobster or Crab Sauce

2 tablespoons olive oil

1 pound lobster or crab shells

2 medium yellow onions, peeled and coarsely diced

2 large carrots, cut into chunks

2 stalks celery, cut into chunks

3 cloves garlic

2 tablespoons tomato paste

1 cup dry sherry

1 cup sweet sherry

3 whole black peppercorns

2 bay leaves

fresh herb stems

Melissa Kelly, the James Beard Award-winning chef of Primo in Rockland, Maine, Tucson, Arizona, and Orlando, Florida, contributed this recipe to the revised edition of Marjorie Standish's classic *Cooking Down East: Favorite Maine Recipes* (Down East Books, 2011). It is a quick, easy recipe to make when you have leftover lobster or crab shells. It can be used as a base for many recipes and it freezes well.

Heat the oil in a stock pot over high heat until smoking. Add the shells and sear in oil, being careful not to burn. Add the onions, carrots, and celery, and sauté until they begin to soften. Add the garlic and sauté for another 2 minutes. Add the tomato paste and sear in the fat as well. Coat shells with tomato without burning (you may have to turn the heat down at this point). Add both sherries and deglaze the pan by using the liquid to remove any bits and pieces that are stuck. Continue cooking until the sherry is reduced and the pan is almost dry. Add the peppercorns, bay leaves, some fresh herb stems, and water, and bring to a boil. Turn it down to a simmer and let this go for at least 1 hour. Taste. In several batches, take a portion of it and very carefully purée in a blender, shells and all. Only fill the blender halfway and pulse so that it doesn't build too much steam. (I usually place a towel over the top of the blender top for safety precautions.) Once all the

2 quarts water

salt and freshly
ground black pepper

sauce has been blended, strain it through a fine mesh strainer or cheesecloth, so as to remove the remaining bits of shell. Season with salt and pepper and reserve for future use, or reduce until desired consistency and flavor. Whisk in a couple tablespoons of butter for a delicious sauce or finish with a splash of heavy cream. Makes 1½ quarts.

Who's Who in Maine Lobsters

DOWNEAST LOBSTERMEN'S ASSOCIATION
downeastlobstermen.org

The DELA was formed in 1991 to address the needs and concerns of lobstermen fishing in eastern Maine, whose fishing grounds present unique challenges owing to their extreme tides.

GULF OF MAINE LOBSTER FOUNDATION
1 High Street, Kennebunk, ME 04043
gomlf.org

The organization involves lobstermen and scientists in research. Its projects have included a rope exchange that helped lobstermen comply with a federal law requiring them to convert to sinking lines and a program to recover and dispose of derelict traps.

LOBSTER INSTITUTE
210 Rogers Hall, University of Maine, Orono, ME 04469
lobsterinstitute.org

The Lobster Institute works with the lobster industry from New York to Newfoundland to sustain a viable lobster fishery through conservation, outreach, research, and education.

MAINE LOBSTER COUNCIL
2 Union Street (Suite 204), Portland, ME 04101
lobsterfrommaine.com

Founded by the lobster industry and funded by lobster license holders, the Maine Lobster Council markets and promotes the sale of Maine lobster to customers worldwide.

MAINE LOBSTERMEN'S ASSOCIATION
21 Western Ave. # 1, Kennebunk, ME 04043
mainelobstermen.org

Founded in 1954, the MLA represents 1,200 member lobstermen on issues related to management, research, and promotion of the fishery.

THE LOBSTER CONSERVANCY
P.O. Box 235, Friendship, ME 04547
lobsters.org

TLC involves fishermen and volunteers in studying the life of lobsters "from egg to plate" in order to gather information that will help sustain a thriving lobster fishery in the Gulf of Maine.

Laurence Parent